Table of Contents

PREFACE I

CHAPTER ONE:
Giving vs. Receiving 1

    POSITIVE ACTIONS REQUIRED:
    Overcoming Any Negatives of Giving from Your Heart
    Love Your Neighbor as Yourself 12

    VOLUNTEERING 13

CHAPTER TWO:
The Power of the Subconscious 15

CHAPTER THREE:
The Perfect Life 19

    LOVE 24

    PERFECT SEXUAL INTERCOURSE 26

CHAPTER FOUR:
Overcoming the Greatest Human Fear 29

CHAPTER FIVE:
The Negatives of Humankind's Deception to a Self-Imposed
Death Sentence...31

CHAPTER SIX:
Positively a Near Perfect World.....................................35
    DIETS...35
    WORK...36
    BENEFITS...37
    EDUCATION..38
    COMMUNICATION..38
    TRANSPORTATION...42
    LOVE JUSTICE SYSTEM..43
    CHURCH...46
    RECREATION...47

CHAPTER SEVEN:
Handling Change...49
    MANAGING EXPECTATIONS..93
    ANGER..123
    EXPECTED FUTURE CHANGES..124

CHAPTER EIGHT:
The Positives of Being Thankful...................................133

CHAPTER NINE:
The Positives of Bawling Uncontrollably...........................143

CHAPTER TEN:
The Value of Complaining..147

CHAPTER ELEVEN:
Negatives of Personal Possessions.................................153

CHAPTER TWELVE:
Positive Personal Possessions.....................................155

CHAPTER THIRTEEN:
Complete Positive 157

CHAPTER FOURTEEN:
The Most Common Obstacle 161

CHAPTER FIFTEEN:
The End of the Age 167

ABOUT THE AUTHOR 173

EPILOGUE 176

I am passionate about giving this book away for humankind's benefit. It's a book about the absolute truth I have learned of the perfect life of complete joy and happiness. It was learned through my true life experiences, including unthinking rebellion against my parents' strict Christian faith and upbringing.

Jesus Christ did not leave my side when I did this or walked away from him. I am able to write this book by the compassionate love, saving and healing, grace, mercy and forgiveness of our unconditional loving Lord and Savior, Jesus Christ. I do not write this book to make you feel sorry for me, because God was just in everything that has befallen me; things happened so I could write this book through my true life experiences. Hopefully, no one else will need to make the same mistakes I made to learn the absolute truth of the perfect life. Instead, they can easily make the choice to live the perfect life, and be thankful I made these mistakes to be able to write this book to show others the way.

Thank you to my children for making me aware of my lifelong attitude of never stopping, quitting or giving up at whatever I'm doing. I have never had this conscious thought before. Further thanks to Mark Victor Hansen for his constructive criticism of my original title, The Subconscious Mind Positively Can. It took me two weeks to think of the current title, and it could not be more perfect for this book.

The Kingdom of God is at hand. I thought it good that I declare to you the signs and wonders Jesus Christ has worked for me, and that I do the work of

God as it is revealed in me. First and foremost, let me reveal to you the greatest work God has done for all of humankind, which of course is for me then, as well as yourself. Your awareness will lead you to the signs and wonders of Jesus Christ, which has worked for me personally, too.

Jesus Christ was sent to the Earth to sacrifice himself by dying on a cross, to be raised three days later for the forgiveness of humankind's sins. He ascended into Heaven and is seated at the right hand of the Father. He will come again to judge the living and the dead. "Whosoever believeth in Jesus, should not perish, but have everlasting life." (2 Corinthians 9 verse 15) Thanks be to God for his indescribable gift.

I am Keith, a content eight year old with forty-three years' worth of experience, half physically dead, and a miracle man walking. It is truly wonderful to finally have this belief, which is doing the work of God, in my heart, soul and mind. I have experienced the most positive events that could ever have happened in my life. In John 6, verses 28 and 29 [28], they said to him, "What shall we do, that we may work the works of God?" [29] Jesus answered and said to them, "This is the work of God that you believe in him whom he sent." For the third most positive, God granted Satan his request that he could be my teacher; the moment after God planted the idea, I would be a peacemaker, in my heart, soul and mind when I was four years old, because God knew it was the only way. He knew I would perfectly learn through true life experiences. It is the absolute truth to the perfect life of complete joy and happiness that we all seek, desire and are required to be living now, at the end of the age.

Satan wanted to be sure I would not live long enough to be God's peacemaker, because I am not a peacemaker on Earth alone, but in all of God's created universe. Satan made me do things that were so foolish and downright stupid. My earthly life required being saved from death, or at least serious physical injury, twenty-eight times, resulting in me becoming completely self-centered, conceited, arrogant, unthankful, unloving and proud. For example, I had an extremely swollen head by these thoughts of myself. Matthew 23 verse 12: "And whoever exalts himself will be abased, and he who humbles himself will be exalted."

For the second most positive, in January of 2006, I was stepping onto Kirkbridge Drive to cross over to the north side when a half-ton truck's side rear-view mirror was so close to my left cheek, I felt the wind from it. To this day, this cheek on the half physically dead side of my body only feels pain or super-hyper sensations. I was standing there trembling, thinking, I would have been decapitated if I had completed stepping onto Kirkbridge Drive. The most overwhelming feelings of puppy love for Jesus Christ came over me, which started the moment I said from my heart, "Thank you Jesus for saving my life." He enabled me to do only one thing.

God has given me the ability to do on my own, choosing with my free will. This is the same free will given to every human being to love God, repent sins and believe God raised Jesus Christ from the dead for everlasting life (2 Corinthians 9 verse 15). Thanks be to God for his indescribable gift. It is hard to imagine that anything could possibly be more positive than this, other than telling you now how you too should have everlasting life. Consider Luke 6 verse 35: "But love your enemies, do good and lend, hoping for nothing in return; and your reward will be great, and you will be sons of the Highest. For He is kind to the unthankful and evil."

I could not stand such intense and overwhelming feelings of puppy love after feeling it constantly for three months. At the beginning of April, 2006, I made the decision that I wanted this love to mature into being in a giving from my heart, true love-faith relationship with Jesus Christ. By the truth, I know of the joy and happiness that you live if you are in a giving from your heart true love relationship with another person. A fine example was Teri Berry's giving from her heart true love for me. This is the kind of love Jesus told us we must have for him to be his disciple, as in Luke 14 verse 26: "If anyone comes to me and hate not his father and mother, wife and children, brothers and sisters, yes, and his own life also, he cannot be my disciple."

This decision made me remember the idea I had the day after my confirmation on December 10, 1978. I had always thought my parents' daily devotional readings were not correct, because they decided what to read from a booklet written by a human being, but this was just an excuse to not participate. That morning I did participate and the readings were from Luke 4 verse 17: "And he was handed the book of the prophet Isaiah. And when he had opened the book, he found the place where it was written…" This caught my attention, making me think, 'If I ever have daily devotional readings, I will pray that Jesus guides my fingers to open the Bible, your word, to the scripture passage you want me to read, as your message to me today. Please provide me with a clear, open and understanding heart, soul and mind of all I read; so I may understand to know the meaning and or relevance to my life; in Jesus name I pray, amen.'

My brother Mark and I knew each other so well, including what the other would think, say and do in any situation encountered in life. Mark passed on, on December 25, 2008, to be free from his life of strength, pain, suffering and understanding to be with Jesus in Heaven. Jesus has taught me through my daily devotional readings to understand what he would think, say and do in any situation I now encounter in my life. John 11 verses 35 and 36 say, [35] "Jesus wept. [36] Then the Jews said, 'See how he loved him!'" In addition, he has taught me to understand the vivid description of the events of the end of the age written throughout the Bible to restore the Earth to its created beauty and splendor that is to begin any moment now.

I have also been taught the understanding of human sexuality, which is the deepest, innermost desire in our lives. In Genesis 3 verse 11, he said: "Who told you that you were naked? Have you eaten from the tree of which I commanded you that you should not eat?" And the first most positive, I lost the majority of my life of love for mammon, which is money, worldly material personal possessions, the visible physical human body and that I, Keith Listoe, am great enough to do everything on my own. On Thursday September six 2007, this was the day after cooking a big birthday dinner for my son Tyler and my other two children. I read Luke 14 verse 13 But when you give a feast, invite the poor, the maimed, the lame, the blind. I immediately decided I would cook a feast for 5 homeless people here in Winnipeg, Mb. because I could seat six at my table.

only to soon think I do not feel right to feed them and let them leave with only a full belly, what could I possibly offer to homeless people in the short term to begin with, my first thoughts were possibly to do their laundry, if I could talk them into staying overnight this would be possible to wash and dry them while they slept, but would then require buying them tooth brushes for the morning. I really wanted to do this thinking what else may I need to have these 5 sleep over. I would need five air mattresses for them to sleep on.

Matthew 7 verses 1 and 2 1 "Judge not, that you be not judged. 2 For with what judgment you judge, you will be judged; and with the same measure you use, it will be measured back to you. This was my reading on Friday September seven 2007.

On Saturday September eight 2007, I read Matthew 19 verse 21 Jesus said to him, "If you want to be perfect, go, sell what you have and give to the poor, and you will have treasure in heaven; and come, follow Me." I thought and prayed what the combined readings meant. I concluded that homeless people might want to hurt me to take my abundant possessions and if I sold my possessions, except what I required to cook and serve the feast, it would provide me more floor space in my apartment to set up the five air mattresses. I placed an ad in the Winnipeg free Press to sell my possessions. I did not sell one item before my planned date of the next Friday, September fourteen 2007. I also did not know where to go to find any homeless people to ask to come to my feast. I decided to change the feast to a Thanksgiving feast. I had not sold a single item before Thanksgiving, but only completed making a priced list of my 169 possessions I was hoping to sell. I changed it to be a Christmas dinner feast instead! I became distracted with the nine day eight night south Florida vacation package for two with my brother Mark that I had arranged to be able to watch a space shuttle launch on December six 2007. I made an appointment with Salvation Army after I returned from this vacation to pick up my possessions as a donation, because I did not feel I required the cash, from selling them, but just wanted to have a clean empty apartment to hold the feast in! I decided to ask five people at the LUM to come to my Christmas dinner feast. I know now the error I made was handing out a list of questions to determine who might benefit the most by attending my feast, because this was being judgmental! Matthew 16 verse 25 it reads,

"For whoever desires to save his life will lose it, and whoever loses his life for My sake will find it."

John 15 verse 5 goes on to say, "I am the vine, you *are* the branches. He who abides in Me, and I in him, bears much fruit; for without Me you can do nothing." It took this kind of magnitude and that Jesus unquestionably saved my life all these times, to make me stop taking life for granted and to be thankful. Exodus 33 verse 19 says, "Then He said, I will make all of My goodness pass before you, and I will proclaim the name of the Lord before you. I will be gracious to whom I will be gracious, and I will have compassion on whom I will have compassion."

Jesus saved my life when I had four bleeding episodes in my brain due to burst aneurysms in December of 2002; but this was to abase me by making my entire physical brain swell to equal the size of my swollen head of the thoughts of myself. They were too big for my skull, resulting in the neurosurgeon doing something he never imagined he would ever do or that I would survive him doing, which was cutting off the top right quarter of my skull. All of this within a second or two, he claims, of my brain collapsing onto the top of my spinal column, which would have killed me instantly. The simplest way I can describe what happened to me was that I became a baby with thirty-nine years' experience. However, this was to be sure I could have everything revealed to me as Jesus said in Matthew 11 verse 25: "At that time Jesus answered and said, 'I thank you Father Lord of Heaven and Earth because you have hidden these things from the wise and prudent and have revealed them to babes.'"

I misused and abused the miraculous healing and recovery Jesus had working for me. That's when I played goalie in hockey on Sunday, November 13, 2005, which could only have been for my own glory, not glory to God. However, I perceive the truth that Jesus used this opportunity to reveal his love, power and might for his own glory by making me play as well as I did. Here is a hyperlink to a video of me playing in this hockey game: www.keithlistoe.ca/Spiritwood_Reunion.wmv.

Jesus saved my life again when I was a pedestrian struck by an SUV on December 10, 2005. Acts 12 verse 23: "Then immediately an angel of the Lord struck him, because he did not give glory to God. And he was eaten by worms and died." Because of the injuries from the SUV striking me, I am no longer able to skate and play goalie. If all that isn't miracle enough for you, I asked the surgeon who put the artificial left shoulder in where the SUV impacted me, dislocating and crushing the shoulder joint ball. I asked him, "If the impact was hard enough to crush the bone, how much damage did it do to the muscle?" He answered, "The muscle was just mush, I only found two small strands hanging in the back, which I attached to the metal I put into your shoulder with Kevlar sutures." He asked me, "Are you able to put your left hand behind your back?" I answered, "I do not know, I have had no reason to try putting my left hand behind my back." He asked, "Try it now please." I put my left hand behind my back. He exclaimed, "I am astounded. I have never seen or thought it possible to put your hand behind your back with an artificial shoulder, but you can!"

Here's the news clipping of accident details.
(key this into the command line of your browser to view the image on-line!
www.keithlistoe.ca/wfp05-12-10.jpg)

My physiotherapist had me see my neurologist to determine why I was feeling pain in my left shoulder. He did an EMG on it. The technician connected many wires onto my left shoulder, chest and arm. She said, "You will feel a shock when I do the tests." She pushed the button. I felt a shock and she exclaimed, "The waves I am getting should not be possible, I must try another one." After the third time she said, "I must have connected a wire incorrectly." She adjusted every wire and tried again. She said, "I have to get the doctor, because the waves I am getting should not be possible."

The doctor came in and pushed the button. He said, "You are correct, it should not be possible, but they definitely are H waves that are only possible to get from an infant. I thought, *now I know how I can move this arm. Jesus replaced all of the mushed muscle with infant's muscle.* You might question how I can have such confidence that Jesus saved my life. I went into the hospital with the most intensely painful headache I had ever felt and learned after my arrival it was due to bleeding in my brain. During an emergency operation to stop the bleeding, they discovered a large blood clot from a prior bleeding three days before, which would have been the reason for a headache on the previous Friday night while playing hockey. They also discovered an uncountable number of aneurysms. A second emergency operation was performed a couple of days later after a third bleed. A couple of days later, the neurosurgeon who performed these operations told my parents that I would not survive another bleed, but I would survive another operation to repair the uncountable aneurysms.

This man had to leave Winnipeg for a meeting that day, so that evening they had to call in another neurosurgeon to perform a third emergency operation after a fourth bleed, causing my entire brain to start swelling, not just in the areas of my brain where the bleeds had already occurred. God used these bleeds to abase me by making my entire physical brain swell to equal the thoughts of myself, a swollen head that was too big for my skull. This resulted in the neurosurgeon doing something he never imagined he would ever do, or that I would even survive him doing it, which was cutting off the top right quarter of my skull to allow my brain to swell without increasing the pressure in my skull.

The neurosurgeon was astounded when I survived. Mom immediately phoned my younger sister Deborah, who had driven to Winnipeg, Mb. From Wetaskiwin, Ab., staying at my place, to search for some olive oil and bring it to the hospital ASAP. When Deborah arrived at the hospital, Mom took the oil and she and my Dad and Deborah went into the ICU to pray for me while I was being prepped for surgery. Mom anointed me with the oil and they prayed for me with the laying on of hands as written in Mark 16 verses 17 and 18 17: "And these signs will follow those who believe: In My name they will cast out demons; they will speak with new tongues; [18] they will take up serpents; and if they drink anything deadly, it will by no means hurt them; they will lay hands on the sick, and they will recover."

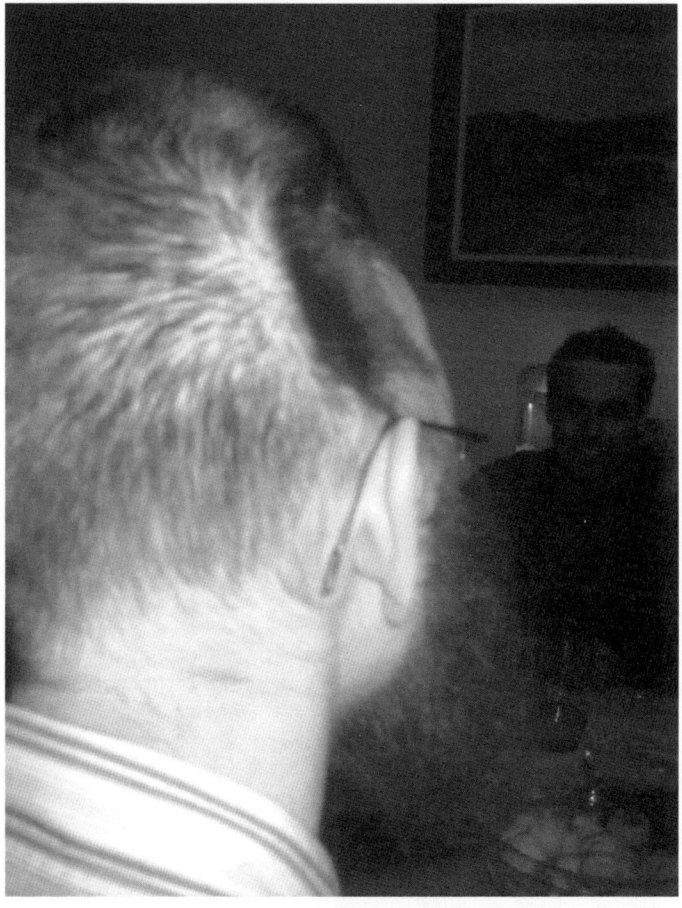

The amount of my skull removed and my new friend George Braz!
(key this into the command line of your browser to view the image on-line!
www.keithlistoe.ca/09-03-12-keith.jpg)

The clearest memory I have in the hospital was thinking the window was open in the wintertime because my left foot was unbearably frozen, regardless of the number of heated sheets they put over it. They ran out of heated sheets. I feel this unbearable frozenness on the left side of my body, even if there is the slightest of cool air, whether I am sitting or sleeping. The second clearest memory I have in the hospital was in the step down unit after the third emergency operation. I looked at the wall, seeing a sign pinned above my head that read: do not lie on right side. The nurse came in asking me if I would like to know and see what had been done to me for this sign to be hung above my head. I said, "Yes." She brought in a mirror, explaining the doctor had cut off the top right quarter of my skull to allow my brain to swell without increasing the pressure in my skull more than it already was. I could see this large lump in the dent of my skull in the mirror on the table over my bed. I decided it must be my brain swelling out of where the bone had been removed from my skull. I wondered if I would be able to feel my brain through my scalp. I gently rubbed my fingers over the lump in the dent of my skull, being surprised to feel tube-like bumps under my scalp. I stopped when I was shocked when something inside my skull could feel my fingers rubbing on it. I was upset and disappointed when I learned from my brother Mark after I was discharged from the hospital on April 7, 2003, that they stopped him from taking a picture of my head with the lump visible in it.

My brother Mark, who was the second most supportive person in the hospital
with me for four months! (key this into the command line of your browser
to view the image on-line! www.keithlistoe.ca/Mark_and_Keith.jpg)

Teri Berry was the number one most supportive person
with me through 2002-now!
(key this into the command line of your browser to view the image on-line.
www.keithlistoe.ca/teri_and_keith3.jpg)

In an MRI review appointment in April of 2005, the neurosurgeon walked into the room carrying the images exclaiming, "I am astounded you survived, let alone recovered at all with the amount of brain damage you have." He explained all the colors in the images, saying, "As you can see, it is very obvious that the majority of the right side of your brain is damaged I can only guess you had too much brain to begin with!"

In 2 Corinthians 8 verses 10 and 11, it states, [10] "And in this I give my advice: It is to your advantage not only to be doing what you began and were desiring to do a year ago; [11] but now you also must complete the doing of it, that as there was the readiness to desire it, so there also may be a completion out of what you have." In truth, I perceive, you seek and desire to be in a giving from your heart, true love, faith relationship with Jesus Christ and giving from your heart love your neighbor as yourself. A life of complete giving from your heart love, which is a life of complete joy and happiness, is the perfect life! Jesus told us repeatedly what to do to live this perfect life. Therefore, you will definitely live this life by becoming a disciple of Jesus Christ. The perfect way to do this is by using the Christ's on-demand daily devotional readings WebApp, I hired someone to code for me here: www.ondemandwisdom.com/Daily_Devotional_Readings.htm.

Love,
Keith Listoe

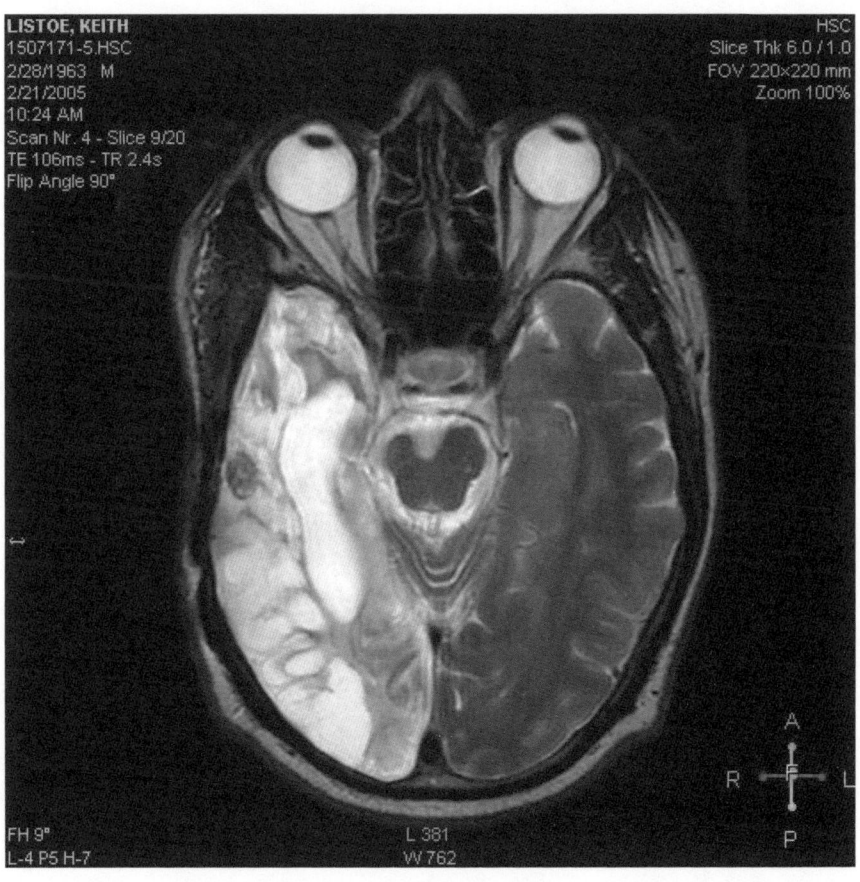

LISTOE, KEITH | HSC
1507171-5.HSC | Slice Thk 6.0 / 1.0
2/28/1963 M | FOV 220×220 mm
2/21/2005 | Zoom 100%
10:24 AM
Scan Nr. 4 - Slice 9/20
TE 106ms - TR 2.4s
Flip Angle 90°

FH 9° | L 381
L-4 P5 H-7 | W 762

MRI 2005/02/21
(Key this into the command line of your browser to view the
image on-line! www.keithlistoe.ca/Halfhead.jpg)

The Perfect Life!

†

CHAPTER ONE

Giving Vs. Receiving

The only one thing in life you instantly receive is the joy and happiness from a true giving heart. Meaning, if you give from your heart, you will instantly receive joy and happiness in your heart, soul and mind. This is something in life that cannot be bought with any amount of money, but may be received by giving to those in need. The more given, the more received. If I am approached by a panhandler now, I first introduce Jesus Christ and myself to them. I then explain lovingly that I do not carry any cash with me, but if you tell me what you need the money for, I might be able to help you personally buy it with my debit card! I have only had two people refuse saying just give me some money. This has made me conclude they only want the money for a bad habit addiction they have. Being able to do this on my walks downtown during my lunch break was the greatest positive of working downtown in the new Manitoba Hydro Place Head Office. With all of the changes combined that have occurred in my life since 2012, I no longer get to enjoy this joy and happiness now working downtown.

1. I am now debt broke, because I miss gave too much in 2010-2012 to six different entities. It was all great learning experiences that will benefit myself and others in the future, by the will of God!

2. I use my short thirty-five minute lunch break to rest my eyes to avoid a headache from working on a computer all day long. The only time a person will not receive this joy and happiness is if they expect some recognition for giving. They may feel some joy and happiness on receiving this recognition; but it pales in comparison to the joy and happiness received with no expectations. A true philanthropist best represents this. Consider Matthew 6 verses 3 and 4, 3 "But when you do a charitable deed, do not let your left hand know what your right hand is doing, 4 that your charitable deed may be in secret; and your Father who sees in secret will Himself reward you openly."

The true want of this giving is not the recognition from others for your giving, but simply the joy and happiness received in your heart soul and mind. If this is all that is sought for, for this giving there will never be the same positive of receiving as giving.

However, receiving without asking or expecting is positive, but still pales in comparison to the positive of giving, especially without being asked to give. I was in the habit of introducing Jesus Christ and myself to people on my bus rides to or home from work. There was a man who boarded the bus on Chancellor at Gaylene and he would frequently sit on the right side seat in front of me, but had never looked in my direction to get his attention to make my introduction. In the spring of 2009, he did look at me and I made my introduction. I learned that his name was George Braz, a brother in Christ and we exchanged contact information. Shortly after this he stopped getting on the bus. I phoned him to inquire what had happened. I learned that he was immigrating to Canada from Brazil and had problems with his lawyer renewing his Visa and he was suspended from his job until he could get it renewed. I could sense that he was the type of man who was determined to do it all on his own and not ask anyone for help or assistance, which is admirable. He was married with a young daughter and his wife was pregnant with their second child and attending the U of M. He was not poor, but in dire straits to support his family. I was in constant prayer for what I should do with the large $5000.00 plus income tax refund I received from my 2008 income taxes. George phoned me one day asking if I would like to go with him and his family to their church, he would come pick me up.

I agreed and immediately said in my heart, "thank you Jesus for letting me know what I can use this money for". I went to the local Christian card shop and bought a nice new friends card. I composed a personal message to include with the $5000 check I wrote to him. He managed to get a new lawyer that successfully renewed his visa and he returned to work. His wife completed her education and delivered a new baby boy. They completed their immigration process. Moreover, one should not refuse to give when asked. Matthew 5 verse 42 "Give to him who asks you, and from him who wants to borrow from you do not turn away." Acts 20 verse 35 "I have shown you in every way, by laboring like this, that you must support the weak. And remember the words of the Lord Jesus, that He said, 'It is more blessed to give than to receive.'"

God wants every human being, or at least the existing church of Christ, to have the ability to make war with the beasts at the end of times, because we know that we are born into the bondage of sin and cannot free ourselves. We must make the firm decision that we want to be in a giving from your heart true love, faith relationship with Jesus Christ, combined with complete trust in God: the Father, the Son, and the Holy Spirit. Jesus told us that if we are in this relationship with him, he will be in us, but this decision enables us to acknowledge that he has always been in us just as he and the Father are one in each other. Giving from your heart is true love. A faith relationship with Jesus Christ, combined with complete trust in God, will result in being able to accept and believe that God has always been in a giving relationship from his heart; it's a true love relationship with you since the moment you were born. John 14 verse 20 "At that day you will know that I am in My Father, and you in Me, and I in you as I am one in my Father and my Father is one in me."

Jesus told us very clearly how he wants us to give to him in Matthew 25 verses 31 to 46:[31] "When the Son of Man comes in His glory, and all the holy angels with Him, then He will sit on the throne of His glory. [32] All the nations will be gathered before Him, and He will separate them one from another, as a shepherd divides *his* sheep from the goats. [33] And He will set the sheep on His right hand, but the goats on the left. [34] Then the King will say to those on His right hand, 'Come, you blessed of My Father, inherit the kingdom prepared for you from the foundation of the world: [35] for I was hungry and you gave Me food; I was thirsty and you gave Me drink; I was a stranger and you took Me in; [36] I *was* naked and you clothed Me; I was sick and you visited Me; I was in prison and you came to Me.' [37] "Then the righteous will answer Him, saying, 'Lord, when did we see You hungry and feed *You,* or thirsty and give *You* drink? [38] When did we see You a stranger and take *You* in, or naked and clothe *You?* [39] Or when did we see You sick, or in prison, and come to You?' [40] And the King will answer and say to them, 'Assuredly, I say to you, inasmuch as you did it to one of the least of these My brethren, you did it to Me.' [41] "Then He will also say to those on the left hand, 'Depart from Me, you cursed, into the everlasting fire prepared for the devil and his angels: [42] for I was hungry and you gave Me no food; I was thirsty and you gave Me no drink; [43] I was a stranger and you did not take Me in, naked and you did not clothe Me, sick and in prison and you did not visit Me.' [44] "Then they also will answer Him, saying, 'Lord, when did we see You hungry or thirsty or a stranger or naked or sick or in prison, and did not minister to You?' [45] Then He will answer them, saying, 'Assuredly, I say to you, inasmuch as you did not do it to one of the least of these, you did not do it to Me.' [46] And these will go away into everlasting punishment, but the righteous into eternal life."

You, too, will enjoy eternal life if you are in such a giving from your heart, true love, faith relationship with Jesus Christ, combined with complete trust in God. You will know for certain that Jesus' words are true. Everything you ask the Father in my name will be given you. 1 John 5 verses 14 and 15 [14] Now this is the confidence that we have in Him, that if we ask anything according to His will, He hears us. [15] And if we know that He hears us, whatever we ask, we know that we have the petitions that we have asked of Him. It's the perfect way to convince yourself that you desire to be in a giving from your heart true love faith relationship with Jesus Christ, combined with complete trust in God. And to love Your neighbor as yourself, is to believe Jesus' words that you should go, sell what you have and give to the poor. If you do this, only keeping what you require to survive, you will become content. You cannot love God and mammon. If you are content, you will want to give in every possible way to your neighbor as he or she requires. Always stay true to whatever decision you make to do good for others, and God will bless you and whomever you decided to do good for with perfect positive results.

After I donated my household possessions to the Salvation Army in December of 2007, I made the decision that I would not buy myself anything unless it is the same or of like value for someone else who really needs it. Consider 1 John 2 verses 15 to 17[15]: Do not love the world or the things in the world. If anyone loves the world, the love of the Father is not in him. [16] For all that is in the world—the lust of the flesh, the lust of the eyes, and the pride of life—is not of the Father but is of the world. [17] And the world is passing away, and the lust of it; but he who does the will of God abides forever."

My three-quarter length leather jacket I had acquired while working for Petro Canada was purchased for me in 1993, when I lost my winter jacket on the road in Mississauga, Ontario. It wore out around the collar, I decided to check getting it repaired by Danier Leather where I bought it, but needed to ask if anyone at the Lutheran Urban Ministry required a winter jacket before I would do this for myself. This was the warmest winter jacket I ever owned and initially I only wore it as my good winter jacket, along with my Gore-Tex bomber jacket I received on the project from Agreevo NA. I had to start wearing my leather jacket only after the bomber jacket was cut off me by the paramedics when the SUV struck me on December 10, 2005. The collar was too worn-out to be repaired by Danier. They also do not sell the three-quarter length leather jackets, so I was out of luck getting myself a new one. However, I learned that Ron at the LUM required a new winter jacket. I initially thought I would buy him one from Danier, because they had a sale on their jackets, but that was not until Christmas and it was already cold outside.

I could not wait until Christmas for the sale for my benefit of buying it cheaper, so I asked Ron if he had a jacket in mind that he thought would be good. He did. I asked him if we could meet at the store, and said I would buy it for him. He told me the jacket was in Bentley Leather in the Portage Place Mall and we agreed to meet there the next evening. I had never been in this store, but from the name I assumed it sold leather jackets. I became worried. I had made a mistake offering to buy him the jacket he wanted without knowing anything about it or the place he wanted to buy it from, because I knew how expensive mine was. I said in my heart, I offered to buy him this jacket, I will not refuse to buy it for him now, regardless of the cost to myself.

We met on Portage Avenue outside the doors into Portage Place Mall. I told Ron I would follow him to the store, because I had no idea where it was. As we were going up the stairs to the second floor, Ron asked me, "Would it be okay if you don't buy me a new jacket, but buy my son a new jacket?" I was speechless to Ron, but in my heart, I said, *I would really like to buy both of them a new jacket, but I must wait to know how much the jacket he wants costs.* As we entered the store, I saw racks of down-filled jackets on sale. I immediately decided, show me the jacket you want to buy for your son and we will go from there. Because they were not leather jackets, I was confident I would be able to buy one for both Ron and his son. After I knew the jacket he picked out for his son was on sale for under $40, I asked him to show me the jacket he wanted for himself. He said, "No I wanted you to buy my son a jacket instead of me". Still, I insisted he show me the jacket he had wanted for himself. His jacket was also on sale, which enabled me to buy them both a jacket cheaper than I thought it was going to cost me to just buy Ron his leather jacket.

I will not go on with my true life experiences to be able to write you this book, but I encourage you to discover being in this giving from your heart true love, faith relationship with Jesus Christ, combined with complete trust in God. The key word in this idea is "in". Jesus used the words, 'you will be in me and I will be in you' in John 14 verse 20: "At that day you will know that I am in My Father, and you in Me, and I in you as I am one in my Father and my Father is one in me." Further, in John 14 verse 10: "Do you not believe that I am in the Father, and the Father in Me? The words that I speak to you I do not speak on My own authority; but the Father who dwells in Me does the works."

What could we possibly not do in Jesus' name if we become as one in God and God one in you? God is love; there is no fear in love. Therefore, if God is in a truly loving relationship with you, you will have absolutely no fear. Let Satan and his beasts be cast to Earth now to deal with such a church of God as the body of Christ! In John 14 verses 12 to 14, it says: [12] "Most assuredly, I say to you, he who believes in Me, the works that I do he will do also; and greater works than these he will do, because I go to My Father. [13] And whatever you ask in My name, that I will do, that the Father may be glorified in the Son. [14]

If you ask anything in My name, I will do it." In 1 Samuel 24 verses 4 and 5, it continues: 4 Then the men of David said to him, "This is the day of which the LORD said to you, 'Behold, I will deliver your enemy into your hand, that you may do to him as it seems good to you.'" And David arose and secretly cut off a corner of Saul's robe. [5] Now it happened afterward that David's heart troubled him because he had cut Saul's robe. More in Matthew 10 verse 28: "And fear not them which kill the body, but are unable to kill the soul: but rather fear him, which is able to destroy both body and soul in hell."

I say we prepare ourselves to take on Satan and his beasts with conditional love. I say conditional because we love every being God created. As such, we want every being God created to return to a loving relationship with Him. To accomplish this with Satan, we must put him between a rock (our Lord and Savior Jesus Christ) and a hard place (Satan's heart). We give Satan the conditions that he must thank God for letting him exist until now. He must openly say, 'I love you, God.' He must tell every human being that they are to worship only God. He must bow his knees to Jesus Christ. If he does not meet these conditions, He is accepting the condition that he loves humankind to the point that he lays down his life so humankind will not be cast into hell fire with him forevermore and we will ask our Father in Heaven in Jesus' name to uncreate Satan. If Satan keeps the conditions, we will only ask our Father in heaven to cast Satan into hell fire forevermore by himself, because Satan is the only being God created who will not be forgiven. Satan will keep the conditions because he thinks he will still be able to fight against God from the hell fire. If he was not afraid to live forevermore in hell fire, he would have ceased moments after rebelling against God. He is afraid of being uncreated for he knows it is impossible for him to do anything more if he does not exist anywhere forevermore.

All things are possible in God through believing in Jesus Christ. Do not let yourselves be afraid of Satan and his beasts. Because he is finally with us at the visible, physical and material surface of life, he has deceived us into loving, to be sure we would not be in a giving from your heart true love, faith relationship with Jesus Christ combined with complete trust in God. Because we have such power in love with God, Satan has been afraid of humankind since the foundation of the world. In 1 John 2 verse 14, it states, "I have written to you, fathers, because you have known Him who is from the beginning. I have written to you, young men, because you are strong, and the word of God abides in you, and you have overcome the wicked one." Satan knows that it is this true love, faith relationship with Jesus Christ, combined with complete trust in God that makes you the god. Jesus said, 'is it not written in your law that you are gods?' In John 10 verse 34, Jesus answered them: "Is it not written in your law, 'I said, "You are gods."' If you make the decision to do good for others and commit yourself to doing something. You then think you made an error in what you said you would do, because it might be more than you thought or anticipated it would be. If you decide in your heart that regardless of the cost to yourself, you will do it. God will ensure the most positive benefits will be acquired for all, including you.

We, too, easily believe in non-personal consequential sayings of Jesus. Like Mark 16 verse 18: "They will take up serpents; and if they drink anything deadly, it will by no means hurt them; they will lay hands on the sick, and they will recover." But to do anything for others that means giving something of value from you are thought of as impossible to do. In Matthew 19 verses 20 to 26, it states: [20] "The young man said to Him, 'All these things I have kept from my youth. What do I still lack?' [21] Jesus said to him, 'If you want to be perfect, go, sell what you have and give to the poor, and you will have treasure in heaven; and come, follow Me.' [22] But when the young man heard that saying, he went away sorrowful for he had great possessions. [23] Then Jesus said to His disciples, 'Assuredly, I say to you that it is hard for a rich man to enter the kingdom of heaven. [24] And again I say to you, it is easier for a camel to go through the eye of a needle than for a rich man to enter the kingdom of God.' [25] When His disciples heard it, they were greatly astonished, saying, 'Who then can be saved?' [26] But Jesus looked at them and said to them, 'With men this is impossible, but with God all things are possible.'"

From personal experience, I assure you this is possible and if you believe Jesus, you will wish you had done this from your youth. If we believe one thing that Jesus said, do not be selective and ignore everything else He said. Jesus only told us what would be the best for us to do to make our lives one with him and our Father in heaven. Luke 16 verses 12 and 13:[12] "And if you have not been faithful in what is another man's, who will give you what is your own? [13] No servant can serve two masters; for either he will hate the one and love the other, or else he will be loyal to the one and despise the other, you cannot serve God and mammon. There are sayings that must be believed in unison to make them possible." Also, in Matthew 5 verses 28 and 29 it says, [28] "But I say to you that whoever looks at a woman to lust for her has already committed adultery with her in his heart. [29] If your right eye causes you to sin, pluck it out and cast it from you; for it is more profitable for you that one of your members perish, than for your whole body to be cast into hell. I say, do not just think of this as looking with your physical vision eyes, but also with your inner eyes of your heart, soul and mind." It continues in Matthew 19 verses 11 and 12[11]: "But He said to them, "All cannot accept this saying, but only those to whom it has been given: [12] For there are eunuchs who were born thus from their mother's womb, and there are eunuchs who were made eunuchs by men, and there are eunuchs who have made themselves eunuchs for the kingdom of heaven's sake. He, who is able to accept it, let him accept it."

I say, it is for those who want to be in a giving from their heart true love faith relationship with Jesus Christ, which is not until death will we part, but until my death that will we be together can accept it. We must only decide what we want and let Jesus' words lead us how to get there. Through further personal experiences, I believe Jesus wants us to give to others from ourselves before asking Him to give to others healing in His name. When I had the financial means, I often went to help out to locations where I know I will find people in need of shelter, food or clothing. If I meet someone in serious need of healing, either at the physical surface of life or at the inner heart, soul and mind's invisible inner, the spirit side of life, I am convinced Jesus is placing me in this location at this time to meet this person. If I will be moved with compassion and mercy for the sick person, to ask with a true believing heart for the person's healing with the laying on of hands. By this we are great witnesses of letting Jesus' love light shine forth through us to help people in their own environment survive now and forevermore! Consider Acts 28 verses 7 to 10: [7] "Now in that region there was an estate of the leading citizen of the island, whose name was Publius, who received us and entertained us courteously for three days. [8] And it happened that the father of Publius lay sick of a fever and dysentery. Paul went in to him and prayed, and he laid his hands on him and healed him. [9] So when this was done, the rest of those on the island who had diseases also came and were healed. [10] They also honored us in many ways; and when we departed, they provided such things as were necessary." And Matthew 5 verse 16: "Let your light so shine before men, that they may see your good works and glorify your Father in heaven."

The key to this is not forcing unbelieving sick people to come to your church facility to attend a service for healing through prayer with the laying on of hands in Jesus' name. Instead, through your faith, go out into their neighborhood, because you are fully mobile and can afford transportation. Once the person is healed, they may want to join you by attending your church for further growth of their faith, which they have been given through Jesus' healing grace and mercy. People on the street living in poverty are no different from rich working people who want to satisfy their wants for pleasure before their needs for survival. Unfortunately, they do not have the luxury of going to the bank for a loan when they spend more than they receive, as working people do. I hope Norman has finally learned this and accepted that if he puts his needs for survival first, he will receive enough on welfare to survive.

Thank God, I was able to take him in off the streets and get him into his own apartment when he refused my offer to take him in to my place in 2010. As in James 4 verses 3 and 4:[3] "You ask and do not receive, because you ask amiss, that you may spend *it* on your pleasures." He also refused my offer of prayer for healing with the laying on of hands in Jesus' name, because I learned after he did request prayer that he is not really paranoid, schizophrenic and sick with Hepatitis C. Instead, he uses this as a way to terrorize people into giving to him, or to be his excuse for his uncontrollable anger when he doesn't get his way and gets arrested. But there is no fear in love, so I called him on his bluff that he wanted to go to church with me by sleeping at his place the first Saturday night. I was there to take him to church with me Sunday morning on the bus, but he refused to go because this also was just his attempt to exploit money from me.

I was successful in scamming him into working for me as my in-person volunteer to make him accept the truth that he is not too disabled to work, but he wants to work and does a very good job at his tasks as a volunteer at the Lutheran Urban Ministry (LUM). He was the most joyful and happy man while he was working for me at the LUM. He also had to accept the truth about the woman he had married. I became 'oh ye of little faith' and incorrectly gave him the money he requested for his addiction. I told him to tell me the truth about what he wanted the money for and to let the truth set him free. I had to stop this incorrect giving when I could not afford it and he ended up in jail because he broke a restraining order his wife had to put on him when he could no longer pay her for sex to support the gang of fourteen kids. He had to learn the hard way that having sex is not the true love required to get married, and getting married does not give him the right to have sex whenever and wherever he wants with his wife.

After I convinced Norman to let me pay his traffic fine in person, as opposed to giving him the $1,800 he asked for to pay it, I was able to conclude near perfectly the events in his life. That's opposed to the lies he told me when I met him that he had lived on the street since he was eleven years old because his mother kicked him out of the house just after his father died. He was in school and living at home until he was in grade ten. He got his driver's license and the people he knew through his mother were not blood relatives, but only members of the gang his father had tried to start when his mother met him.

They all convinced him to steal a car to be used as the getaway vehicle for them to rob a bank. He began to drive recklessly after they were almost caught and the police tried to pull him over. He made the mistake of thinking he could just drive away from them, but it only resulted in his traffic fines and being thrown into prison. I met his mother also and was eventually able to conclude the events in her life, but I did not dare ask her about it because they involved the murder of Norman's father. I was able to make these conclusions by her reaction to one set of questions I asked her. That's after I had to stop giving her money for a drug she claimed she required for her cancer treatment, when she could not provide me with a prescription or receipts for the medication she was buying. My questions were: In what year and how did Norman's dad die? Her answer was, 'I don't know, you would have to ask his stepsister, Kathy.' This was the first time I heard that he had a stepsister. I concluded she had been married to a white man and had this daughter. Kathy was five years old when she started kindergarten. Her Mother felt a sense of freedom now and began an affair with a native man that involved using LSD. She could not afford to pay him cash for the LSD he provided, but accepted payment as having sexual intercourse with her. This resulted in her getting pregnant with Norman. To try to save her marriage, she claimed that she was raped. She continued to see this native man to get his LSD the entire time she was pregnant with Norman, which is the reason for Norman's mental illness. She could not remain in her marriage to the white man through all of this, so she moved in with the native man and had a daughter and another son with him.

When her daughter Kathy was sixteen years old, she thought it would be great to have her try LSD, so Kathy went with her one night to get some. This native man thought his payment would be to have sexual intercourse with Kathy. Her mother walked in on him raping her and killed him with a cast-iron frying pan. She never missed a day using LSD or a similar drug since she got pregnant with Norman, other than during her two subsequent pregnancies, which was why her body looked like she was suffering from cancer. She just recently died, so I am not able to confirm how perfectly I concluded her life events.

POSITIVE ACTIONS REQUIRED:
Overcoming Any Negatives of Giving from Your Heart
Love Your Neighbor as Yourself

If you follow Jesus' instructions to take a stranger in, be certain to clean your place you live in well and often. This means at the least vacuuming weekly or, even better, immediately after each visit from a stranger. When you do your laundry, use hot water to wash your clothes and the hot setting for the dryer to be sure any bed bugs will be naturally killed to prevent an infestation in your living place. It says in Romans 13 verse 8, "Owe no one anything except to love one another, for he who loves another has fulfilled the law." I made the mistake in 2011-2012 of giving more than I had by going into debt, which resulted in me now having to make loan payments that consume any extra money I had to enable me to live the perfect life of complete joy and happiness. But I am confident that this debt will soon be paid off, enabling me to once again live the perfect life of complete joy and happiness of giving from my heart love my neighbor as myself.

VOLUNTEERING

From my personal experiences of finally giving the maximum I can, I now choose to use money as charitable donations. After all, I'm now too disabled to feel comfortable volunteering in person. Therefore, I have come up with the following changes to our current charitable donation: In today's use of technology, a new system could be developed that would print a charitable donation receipt for any in-person volunteering. The person would enter their SIN upon starting to volunteer, then re-enter it to print their receipt at the end of their time. The value of the receipt would be minimum wage times the number of hours volunteered. Welfare recipients would be required to volunteer hours as a full-time job to receive their welfare payments. Again from personal experience of misusing my time, I collected UI by going on a winter vacation. UI recipients would also be required to provide volunteer receipts for hours volunteered as if working full-time to receive UI benefits.

CHAPTER TWO:

The Power of the Subconscious

I believe that we are created in God's image with our own free will to choose who will be in our subconscious mind. Your subconscious will be God if you choose to live a life of love, or the devil if you choose to live a life of sinfulness. I write this because our subconscious mind works at God's speed in instantly knowing every detail of your life. Your subconscious mind is able to produce the required information for our conscious mind to react or think correctly to the current situation. Being our subconscious mind is what enables God to know the exact thoughts of every human being. See 1 Corinthians 6 verses 19 and 20, [19]: "Or do you not know that your body is the temple of the Holy Spirit who is in you, whom you have from God, and you are not your own? 20 For you were bought at a price; therefore glorify God in your body and in your spirit, which are God's." Also John 14 verse 20: "At that day you will know that I am in My Father, and you in Me, and I in you." Matthew 12 verse 25: "But Jesus knew their thoughts, and said to them: "Every kingdom divided against itself is brought to desolation, and every city or house divided against itself will not stand."

The subconscious mind is also aware of the entire universe and its happenings to ensure our conscious mind takes the correct actions at the correct time to be most beneficial to one's neighbors in their life here on Earth, if we choose to live on the love side of life. Consider the following example.

On June 15, 2006, I was registered to partake in a teleconference call hosted by Jack Canfield beginning at 8 p.m. CST. I had created a reminder including the phone number to call and the pass code required. About 7:30 p.m. that evening, my common law spouse Teri's daughter, Koren, came over to use my computer in the basement to complete her income tax, using the phone as well to get the required information. I was not aware of her coming over to do this and had not made backup plans to access the numbers required to be on this teleconference call, or to have my phone voice recorder on another phone. It was connected to the phone in the basement by my computer, which I was planning on using to record this teleconference call. Due to my strokes, I am quite limited in my abilities to multitask now, especially writing notes as I listen to someone talking, so if I want notes, I record the telephone call. However, as 8 p.m. neared, I had the thought to not interrupt her doing her taxes, as I would surely have another opportunity to hear Jack's message on this teleconference call. So I began to work on something else on Teri's new computer upstairs in our living room.

I was feeling very much at ease not being on the call. The following day, I received an e-mail stating that the teleconference call did not occur as the number of callers to hear it overloaded the phone system, which they were very surprised by, so were having a new call on Friday evening. I successfully did it on Friday night, recording the entire call. However, I did not learn anything new on how to be successful, as I have been most successful my entire life, but it was very nice to learn how the subconscious mind knows what all is going on to make your conscious mind think correctly in any given time or situation. One only needs to listen to it. Not that it provides detailed information on what is happening elsewhere in the world, but it does provide the correct thinking to act appropriately to what is happening there.

I experienced another great example of the power of the subconscious on Friday September 5, 2014. Cody made me aware on Thursday September 4, 2014 that his tuition had to be paid by September 10, 2014. I had to get the money transferred out of his RESP to pay it and was worried I would not have sufficient time to complete it before Monday September 8, 2014. I phoned my bank account manager, Kim Hall, Friday morning to get an appointment only with another account manager at 5:00 pm. I made numerous mistakes at work that prevents me from being in the office beyond my regular work hours of 7:00 Am to 3:30 pm. I know there is not sufficient time for me to go home at 3:30 Pm and return to the bank by 5:00 pm for this appointment, I decided to go to the Wal-Mart in the St. Vital mall instead. I missed catching the #55 bus at 3:35 pm. The next bus was not until 3:56 pm that did not provide me sufficient time to do this either. I decided to return to the main floor galley of Manitoba Hydro Place to wait until 5 Pm. As I was waiting I had the idea to go wait in the waiting area of the Royal bank my appointment was in. The account manager, Kim Hall that made the appointment for me, saw me sitting there, saying she had fifteen minutes free that should be enough time to process the withdrawal and transfer.

I believe it is also a direct link to God between every human being here on this Earth. As such, the words 'I am with you every second of the day' are so believable; not that God requires such a connection to be with us, as his powers require nothing to make his will be done! However, from a human brain's ability to understand such a being with, there must be some method through which this is done. As well, the subconscious mind is not a physical tangible thing, but is the part of our minds producing the information to our conscious mind and even controlling the non-conscious actions our body makes in various situations throughout life. That includes anything that occurs without a conscious thought to do it, a reflex reaction, for example. If you are not living on the love side of life, the devil will provide your conscious mind with the incorrect information to misuse the abundant opportunities God provides every human being to do good things for our neighbors, and to use it for their own use specifically becoming completely self-centered, selfish and greedy.

I also believe that the subconscious mind is the mechanism God created to ensure one receives what is asked for by ensuring it wants the conscious mind's thinking to be correct. Further, by praying and asking for something, it moves this conscious asking into the subconscious mind, making it more than likely it will occur for the person asking. You may ask how it works for non-believers who do not pray yet get all they want in life. Well, I believe there is another way to move one's wants and desires into the subconscious mind, making them much more likely to occur. This is done by consciously thinking about what it is you want or desire, then making a conscious decision to achieve these goals. This truly defines the mechanism in every human being to be able to be what one thinks about, not instantly, but over a required period depending on the magnitude of the request. On the other hand, simply put, results are equivalent to the effort put into it, which corresponds to the law of nature that for each action there is an opposite and equal reaction. If nothing is done, nothing is returned.

One must take action of some kind or at some point in time if they desire change in their life. This action is much more than sitting and dreaming or thinking about what you want to be or receive. Nothing in life is given free; get off your butt and take action to receive the return you want or desire. If you think God-centered, your thoughts will be at the correct time to take the correct actions to be beneficial to your family and neighbors before your own prosperity. It is also to your benefit in your heart, soul and mind, by receiving the most joy possible in this life here on Earth. You may question me on God being our subconscious mind to make our conscious mind's thinking correct. For how would God allow people to commit the horrific evil acts they do to other people here on this Earth he created? He created us with our own free will, for if not we would all be simple robot beings making no mistakes of any kind. I am unable to even imagine a world as such for it just has no meaning like our world has. Consider 2 Timothy 1 verse [14] "That good thing which was committed to you, keep by the Holy Spirit who dwells in us," and Luke 6 verses 8 and 9, [8]: "But He knew their thoughts, and said to the man who had the withered hand, "Arise and stand here." And he arose and stood. [9] Then Jesus said to them, "I will ask you one thing: Is it lawful on the Sabbath to do good or to do evil, to save life or to destroy it."

CHAPTER THREE:

The Perfect Life

We humans were deceived into thinking we seek and desire to live a life of pleasure, as opposed to a life of complete joy and happiness. Genesis 3 verses 11 and 12 says, [11] "And He said, "Who told you that you *were* naked? Have you eaten from the tree of which I commanded you that you should not eat?" [12] Then the man said, "The woman whom You gave *to be* with me, she gave me of the tree, and I ate."

The perfect life is a life of complete joy and happiness. A life of complete joy and happiness is only possible as a life of complete giving from your heart love, which is being one in God and God being one in you. Love God and love your neighbor as yourself. See 1 Corinthians 13 verse 12: "And now abide faith, hope, love, these three; but the greatest of these *is* love." I had a very negative experience just after I moved to Winnipeg, Mb. in 1991. I was walking down Portage Avenue and a panhandler requested some money. I know now that I rudely and ignorantly told this man I did not have any money as I kept walking past him. He immediately got up and began to follow me. I thought, great; this is how the people are here in Winnipeg, where I now live! I know I was like this, because I was greedy, selfish, unloving and scared!

There is no love for material personal possessions or the visible physical human body. Jesus told us repeatedly how to live this perfect life. For example, in Mark 12 verses 29 to 31:²⁹ Jesus answered him, "The first of all the commandments *is, 'Hear, O Israel, the LORD our God, the LORD is one.* ³⁰ And you shall love the LORD your God with all your heart, with all your soul, with all your mind, and with all your strength.'"

This is the first commandment. ³¹ And the second, like it, is this, "You shall love your neighbor as yourself." There is no other commandment greater than these. Consider Matthew 25 verses 34 to 36: ³⁴ "Then the King will say to those on His right-hand, 'Come, you blessed of My Father, inherit the kingdom prepared for you from the foundation of the world, ³⁵ for I was hungry and you gave Me food; I was thirsty and you gave Me drink; I was a stranger and you took Me in; ³⁶ I *was* naked and you clothed Me; I was sick and you visited Me; I was in prison and you came to Me.'"

These are good descriptions of how to love your neighbor as yourself. Luke 14 verse 13: "But when you give a feast; invite the poor, the maimed, the lame, the blind." In Luke 16 verse 13, "No servant can serve two masters; for either he will hate the one and love the other, or else he will be loyal to the one and despise the other. You cannot serve God and mammon." Matthew 19 verse 21: Jesus said to him, "If you want to be perfect, go sell what you have and give to the poor, and you will have treasure in heaven; and come, follow Me." Matthew 18 verses 21 and 22"²¹ "Then Peter came to Him and said, 'Lord, how often shall my brother sin against me, and I forgive him? Up to seven times?'" ²² Jesus said to him, "I do not say to you, up to seven times, but up to seventy times seven.'" 1 John 3 verse 17: "But whoever has this world's goods, and sees his brother in need, and shuts up his heart from him, how does the love of God abide in him?" 1 John 2 verse 5: "But whoever keeps His word, truly the love of God is perfected in him. By this we know that we are in Him." 1 John 2 verse 21: "I have not written to you because you do not know the truth, but because you know it, and that no lie is of the truth." I write this by the truth I know from my own true life experiences. In Matthew 6 verse 33: "But seek first the kingdom of God and His righteousness, and all these things shall be added to you." King Solomon wrote it much too simply and concisely to not be overlooked in the entire book of Ecclesiastes. Ecclesiastes 3 verses 12 and 13:¹² "I know that nothing is better for them than to rejoice, and to do good in their lives, ¹³ and also that every man should eat and drink and enjoy the good of all his labor—it is the gift of God." 1 John 3 verse 16: "By this we know love, because He laid down His life for us. And we also ought to lay down our lives for the brethren." To clarify, the life we ought to lay down is our life of love for worldly, material personal possessions and love for the visible, physical human body. The perfect life also includes faith in Jesus Christ for the forgiveness of your sins and salvation unto everlasting life, or complete trust in God. Acts 13 verses 38 and 39:38 "Therefore, let it be known to you, brethren, that through this Man is preached to you the forgiveness of sins; [39] and by Him everyone who believes is justified from all things from which you could not be justified by the law of Moses." John 3 verse 16: "For God so loved the world that He gave His only begotten Son, that whoever believes in Him should not perish but have everlasting life." Have you sold all your personal possessions, except what you require for surviving? Do you have no desire to buy another personal possession because you are content? If you do this, you learn how free your life is of worries, anxiety, stress, and fear. You now understand that because you have everything you require to survive, you are rich. You make your first decision to provide something to a poor, needy person what they require to survive. You have just found the way to a life of complete joy and happiness; the perfect life! It's a life of perfect giving from your heart love, which does not include any partiality or discrimination. I will not say, 'because you are not a white man, I will not love you,' or, 'because you are not a Canadian, I will not love you,' or, 'because you are not a Christian, I will not love you,' or, 'because you are a woman, I will not love you,' or, 'because you are gay, I will not love you'. But I will say, 'I love you enough to offer you prayer for healing with the laying on of hands in Jesus' name.' In 1 John 1 verse 4: "And these things we write to you that your joy may be full." I write these things to you so that your joy may be full like mine is and filling more and more every day! John 13 verse 35: "For this is the message that you heard from the beginning, that we should love one another." God wants every human being, or at least the existing church of Christ, to have the ability to make war with the beasts at the end of times. We know that we are born into the bondage of sin and cannot free ourselves. We must make the firm decision that we want to be in a giving from your heart true love, faith relationship with Jesus Christ, combined with complete trust in God. Jesus told us that if we are in this relationship with him, he will be in you just as he and the Father are one in each other. Being in a giving from your heart true love, faith relationship with Jesus Christ, combined with complete trust in God, will result in God being in a loving relationship with you. John 14 verse 20: "At that day you will know that I am in My Father, and you in Me, and I in you as I am one in my Father and my Father is one in me." John 14 verse 10: "Do you not believe that I am in the Father, and the Father in Me? The words that I speak to you I do not speak on My own authority; but the Father who dwells in Me does the works."

Jesus told us very clearly how he wants us to give to him. Matthew 25 verses 31 to 46:[31] "When the Son of Man comes in His glory, and all the holy angels with Him, then He will sit on the throne of His glory. [32] All the nations will be gathered before Him, and He will separate them one from another, as a shepherd divides his sheep from the goats. [33] And He will set the sheep on His right hand, but the goats on the left. [34] Then the King will say to those on His right hand, 'Come, you blessed of My Father, inherit the kingdom prepared for you from the foundation of the world, [35] for I was hungry and you gave Me food; I was thirsty and you gave Me drink; I was a stranger and you took Me in; [36] I was naked and you clothed Me; I was sick and you visited Me; I was in prison and you came to Me.' [37] "Then the righteous will answer Him, saying, 'Lord, when did we see You hungry and feed You, or thirsty and give You drink? [38] When did we see You a stranger and take You in, or naked and clothe You? [39] Or when did we see You sick, or in prison, and come to You? [40] And the King will answer and say to them, 'Assuredly, I say to you, inasmuch as you did it to one of the least of these My brethren, you did it to Me.' [41] "Then He will also say to those on the left hand, 'Depart from Me, you cursed, into the everlasting fire prepared for the devil and his angels, [42] for I was hungry and you gave Me no food; I was thirsty and you gave Me no drink; [43] I was a stranger and you did not take Me in, naked and you did not clothe Me, sick and in prison and you did not visit Me.' [44] Then they also will answer Him, saying, 'Lord, when did we see You hungry or thirsty or a stranger or naked or sick or in prison, and did not minister to You?' [45] Then He will answer them, saying, 'Assuredly, I say to you, inasmuch as you did not do it to one of the least of these, you did not do it to Me.' [46] And these will go away into everlasting punishment, but the righteous into eternal life."

If you are in a giving from your heart true love, faith relationship with Jesus Christ, combined with complete trust in God, you will know for certain that Jesus' words are true. "Everything you ask the Father in my name will be given you." The strongest and perfect way to convince yourself that you desire to be in such a giving from your heart true love, faith relationship with Jesus Christ, combined with complete trust in God and love your neighbor as yourself is to believe Jesus' words that you should go, sell what you have and give to the poor. If you do this, only keeping what you require to survive you will become content. You cannot love God and mammon. If you are content, you will want to give in every possible way. You are now able to give to your neighbor as he or she requires.

Always stay true to whatever decision you make to do good for others, and God will bless you and whomever you decided to do good for with perfect positive results. They'll be in more abundance than you thought you were ever going to do. I will not go on with my true life experiences to be able to write you this book, but encourage you to discover being in a giving from your heart true love, faith relationship with Jesus Christ, combined with complete trust in God. The key word in this idea is "in". Jesus used the words 'you will be in me and I will be in you.' John 14 verse 20: "At that day you will know that I am in My Father, and you in Me, and I in you as I am one in my Father and my Father is one in me." John 14 verse 10: "Do you not believe that I am in the Father, and the Father in Me? The words that I speak to you I do not speak on My own authority; but the Father who dwells in Me does the works."

What could we possibly not do in Jesus' name if we become as one in God and God one in you? Go forth in a giving from your heart true love-faith relationship with Jesus Christ, combined with complete trust in God! God is love; there is no fear in love. Therefore, if God is in a loving relationship with you, you will have absolutely no fear. Let Satan and his beasts be cast to Earth now to deal with such a church of God as the body of Christ! John 14 verses 12 to 14:[12] "Most assuredly, I say to you, he who believes in Me, the works that I do he will do also; and greater works than these he will do, because I go to My Father. [13] And whatever you ask in My name, that I will do, that the Father may be glorified in the Son. [14] If you ask anything in My name, I will do it." 1 Samuel 24 verses 4 and 5: [4] "Then the men of David said to him, "This is the day of which the LORD said to you, 'Behold, I will deliver your enemy into your hand, that you may do to him as it seems good to you.' And David arose and secretly cut off a corner of Saul's robe. [5] Now it happened afterward that David's heart troubled him because he had cut Saul's robe."

LOVE

Let's define the verb love:

To have a great affection or liking for:
"I love French food!"; "She loves her boss and works hard for him."
Derives or receive pleasure from; get enjoyment from; take pleasure in:
"I love cooking."
Be enamored or in love with:
"She loves her husband deeply."
Have sexual intercourse:
"They made love in the back of the car."

Let's define the noun:

A strong positive emotion of regard and affection:
"Children need a lot of love."; "his love for his work."
Any object of warm affection or devotion:
"The theatre was her first love."
Someone who is loved (used as term of endearment).
A deep feeling of sexual desire and attraction:
"She was his first love."; "Their love left them indifferent to their surround-ings."
A score of zero in tennis or squash:
"It was 40-love."
Sexual activities (often including sexual intercourse) between two people.
"He hadn't had any love in months."; "He has a very complicated love life."; "His sexual love disgusted her."; "His making love disgusted her".

Love can be British informal term as a friendly form of address. It is this misconceived ideas of love that is the reason Satan wanted to be sure Eve and Adam ate from the Tree of Knowledge of good and evil, as written in Genesis 3 verses 11 and 12: [11] "And He said, 'Who told you that you were naked? Have you eaten from the tree of which I commanded you that you should not eat?'" [12] Then the man said, "The woman whom you gave to be with me, she gave me of the tree, and I ate." True love does not include anything of a sexual nature, but only to do good for others that they have everything they require to survive now and forevermore! Unless you have been true to yourself in keeping your visible physical body private and concealed until after you have made the decision in your heart, soul and mind to marry another person, because your emotional, intellectual and spiritual needs are satisfied in your relationship together. Then, after you have discussed in detail your thoughts of parenting, the female of the relationship will initiate the onset of sexual activities on the first ovulation post your marriage. You have agreed to start a family because the female's desire for sexual intercourse is at its highest level, which is the reason for so many unwanted pregnancies of unmarried couples.

This is the true meaning of marriage in the sight of God, the judge who will result in a marriage of until death; we will not part that will to also include the enjoyment of sexual intercourse well into your senior years, which you truly seek and desire. John 13 verses 16 and 17:[16] "Most assuredly, I say to you, a servant is not greater than his master; nor is he who is sent greater than he who sent him. [17] If you know these things, happy are you if you do them." John 15 verses 11 to 13:[11] "These things I have spoken to you, that My joy may remain in you, and that your joy may be full. [12] This is My commandment, that you love one another as I have loved you. [13] Greater love has no one than this, than to lay down one's life for his friends. [14] You are My friends if you do whatever I command you." 1 Timothy 6 verses 6 to 9 [6] "But godliness with contentment is great gain. [7] For we brought nothing into this world, and it is certain we can carry nothing out. [8] And having food and clothing, with these we shall be content. [9] But those who desire to be rich fall into temptation and a snare, and into many foolish and harmful lusts which drown men in destruction and perdition. 1 Timothy 6 verses [17] to 19 [17]: "Command those who are rich in this present age not to be haughty, nor to trust in uncertain riches but in the living

God, who gives us richly all things to enjoy. [18] Let them do good, that they be rich in good works, ready to give, willing to share, [19] storing up for themselves a good foundation for the time to come, that they may lay hold on eternal life.

Proverbs 14 verse 21 He who despises his neighbor sins; But he who has mercy on the poor, happy is he.   Nehemiah 8:10 Then he said to them, "Go your way, eat the fat, drink the sweet, and send portions to those for whom nothing is prepared; for this day is holy to our Lord. Do not sorrow, for the joy of the LORD is your strength.

PERFECT SEXUAL INTERCOURSE

Having simultaneous ejaculation orgasms is perfect sexual intercourse; this is only possible with the correct perfect foreplay. It is only my theory because my parents are unwilling to communicate to confirm that my theory is correct about their sexual experiences. But my Mom did answer two point blank questions of her sexual experiences from near the beginning of their marriage, which has resulted in them being sexually addicted to each other.

I was able to conclude this theory because of my Mothers incorrect instructions of do not have sex in my youth. I write incorrect, because having sex is our deepest innermost desire in life that is the reason all advertising uses sex in it to convince people to buy their product, but instills in our children that sex is OK to just have. I made an equally incorrect error in not saying anything to my children about sex. I write this subchapter now, so all who read it might decide to make the correct choice to refrain from having sex until after you have made the decision in your heart, soul and mind to marry another person, because your emotional, intellectual and spiritual needs are satisfied in your relationship together!

This addiction has enabled them to remain married for over fifty years now! Being sexually addicted to the person you have married enables you to overlook the things you learn to dislike about your spouse. There is no comparison between the individual pleasure experienced from individual orgasms opposed to the mutual ecstasy experienced from perfect sexual intercourse! This is a gift from God if you so choose to be in a giving from your heart true love, faith relationship with Jesus Christ and refrain from exposing your naked body to anyone before you have made the decision in your heart, soul and mind to marry another person, because your emotional, intellectual and spiritual needs are satisfied in your relationship together! However, because we all make mistakes and the perfect life is a choice, one may choose to live this perfect life and enjoy perfect sexual intercourse well into your senior years in a human marriage relationship that is until death we will not part! I love the woman Teri Berry too much to ask her to marry me to prove my theory personally, because I have decided to move to Israel and become a Jew to become the universal peacemaker I was created to be and this would mean she would move with me that would mean she could not be with her children and grandchildren. Since I decided I wanted the overwhelming and intense feelings of puppy love for Jesus Christ, mature into being in a giving from my heart true love, faith relationship with Jesus Christ in April of 2006, I have not felt lonely the slightest, but have never felt more fulfilled in a relationship! I am convinced had my parents taught me this truth of true giving from your heart love relationships prior to my puberty, I would be in a perfect marriage relationship now not divorced. Being sexually addicted to the person you have married will result in you being committed, gentle kind, caring, patient and responsible, to be sure you can have what you are addicted to. I think this is the only addiction that is from God for good. Matthew 19 verses 5 and 6 5 and said, 'For this reason a man shall leave his father and mother and be joined to his wife, and the two shall become one flesh'? 6 So then, they are no longer two but one flesh. Therefore what God has joined together, let not man separate."

CHAPTER FOUR:

Overcoming the Greatest Human Fear

The greatest human fear is death. The average human being is much too uncomfortable to even talk about it. Yes, this greatest fear is death. Yes, there is a way to overcome this fear. First and foremost, find true belief in our Lord and Savior Jesus Christ, followed by being in a giving from your heart true love-faith relationship with Jesus Christ, combined with complete trust in God. Once you have both of these in your heart, soul and mind, you will not just overcome your fear of death, but look forward to your death to be gone from this life of human weakness and misunderstanding and in the kingdom of God with Jesus Christ. It's the ultimate positive possible. This, however, is a very self-centered way of overcoming your fear of death. If you are not self-centered, you will not so easily overcome your fear of death, because you will fear dying before you know that your loved ones and friends have this loving believing relationship with Jesus Christ, to have everlasting life with you in the kingdom of God.

CHAPTER FIVE:

The Negatives of Humankind's Deception to a Self-Imposed Death Sentence

Humankind has created one thing in the visible material surface of life that prevents us from saving lives. It is so evident when we all want to help when natural disasters occur. It also prevents the countries with the food resources from providing assistance to those in need around the world. A high-level overview of the results of the death sentence makes it easy to understand the problems worldwide, from the lowest level within every home to the macro level between every country. The death sentence is perpetuated by greed, selfishness, discrimination, oppression, envy, covetousness, pride and arrogance.

At the lowest level, we cannot assist those in need to survive in our cities. It is so near to everyone who has the financial means to assist those in their own cities. Every person's greed and selfishness prevents them from allowing their true feelings of love to take over to help their fellow human beings. However, when it is a natural disaster on the other side of the world, all too many people express how badly they feel for the people hurt. They feel great that they are openly expressing their feelings as it appears they have love in them for others' well-being. But, in reality, it is only easily expressed, because the disaster is so far away that the possibility of having an actual personal impact on them is minuscule when compared to helping even a single person in their own city.

I see how countries are similar to human beings individually. Numerous individuals have the privilege of acquiring more money than they could possibly ever use for their survival. They refuse to accept the truth that the only thing all the money has brought into their lives is worries, anxiety, stress and fear; they worry that someone else might do something to steal some of their money, or harm them or their children for some of their money or the personal possessions they have acquired with the money. They hire personal guards and install such extensive alarm systems that they might as well live in a prison. They have all of these bodyguards because they are scared.

I see the countries that have had the privilege to amass more wealth than they know what to do with, except brag and show-off worldwide about how great they think their countries are. They are developing such extensive security systems at any point of entry into their countries that the country itself is like a prison. It is becoming the norm that their citizens are attacked when they go into other countries. Instead of using their mass of wealth to help and assist others worldwide to save lives, they use it to develop extreme war machines to kill people in any other countries that do not follow their demands.

In time of war, no government is ever strapped for cash to build weapons. If governments would spend the same amount of cash and time on natural disasters, the people dying could more rapidly be rescued and lives could be saved. It is a sad state of humankind that we can only spend unlimited money to kill other human beings, as opposed to saving them. I say the true test of a Country's citizens would be to reverse the funding of humanitarian efforts to feed the starving, shelter the homeless and cure the ills of the world, instead of going to war with another country. We all know that insufficient funds are donated to save many lives worldwide. The great military training and organization of setting up living and hospital requirements for the front-line troops would serve well at natural disasters, where shelter, food, water, sanitation and medical treatment are so badly needed. I would like to see the greatest superpower on Earth do this because of an unlimited amount of love, care, protection and lifesaving as opposed to who has the most money and military might.

If a natural disaster area is not approachable on land or sea, the military could utilize paratroop capabilities to provide rescue assistance for fast deployment of hospital, water, food and sanitation. Orderly distribution of water and food could be set up with military precision. The military's main function becomes the saving of lives in natural disasters.

Money is humankind's self-imposed death sentence. If it is not apparent now, it definitely will be at the end of times. Consider Revelation 13 verses 16 and 17:16 "He causes all, both small and great, rich and poor, free and slave, to receive a mark on their right hand or on their foreheads, 17 and that no one may buy or sell except one who has the mark or the name of the beast, or the number of his name." The following Bible verse Philippians 2 verse 3: "Let nothing be done through selfish ambition or conceit, but in lowliness of mind let each esteem others better than himself." This would be a great start to overcome this death sentence. In today's day and age, humankind has the means and ability to provide everything required for survival to every human being worldwide! Unthinkably, we refuse to even try to do so, because of the self-imposed death sentence of money!

CHAPTER SIX:

Positively a Near Perfect World

1 John 1 verse 8: "If we say that we have no sin, we deceive ourselves, and the truth is not in us." Because of this, it is impossible for humankind to make the perfect world. We must determine the ways to be able to free ourselves from Satan's deception of the meaning, value and power of love, to the visible physical and material surface of life opposed to the invisible heart, soul and mind inner spirit side of life, which results in these, worries, anxiety, stress and fear. At the highest level, we are in bondage to greed and selfishness, jealousy, envy, covetousness fornication, adultery, stealing lying and murder.

DIETS

Because of this, I see an increased problem of human beings overeating with free food, and the levels of obesity will increase exponentially. I see today's diets causing more worries, anxiety and stress over what must not be eaten, which causes more harm to a person than a few extra pounds. The reason for extra pounds is not what you eat, but how much you eat. There will be serious repercussions when items of any kind go out of stock. This will be the first growing pain to overcome: the incredible increase in demand for food. The love for the visible physical human body that results in fornication, adultery, lying and murder (abortion), is much more difficult to overcome than the love for material, personal possessions.

The perfect life we are able to achieve is by following, 1 John 1 verse 9: "If we confess our sins, He is faithful and just to forgive us our sins and to cleanse us from all unrighteousness." You must believe that Jesus Christ was sent to the Earth to sacrifice himself by dying on a cross, to be raised three days later for the forgiveness of humankind's sins. He ascended into heaven and is seated at the right hand of the Father. He will come again to judge the living and the dead. Whosoever believeth in Jesus should not perish, but have everlasting life! If you have more than this and only use it to buy yourself worldly, material personal possessions, you are filthy rich.

I envision freedom from Satan's deception to love for money and worldly, material personal possessions by replacing money with a single charity survival card system. Every human being will be granted a card to ensure no one receives the mark of the beast at the end of times. I diagnose that the Earth has a terminal illness from the infection of the pollution humankind has contaminated it with in ever increasing abundance throughout history. Because of this, I say, just as a human being diagnosed with a terminal illness, the exact date and time of death is still as unknown as ever, but it is more than likely to be sooner rather than later. The card must be activated for use by working. Every debt and bank account will be eliminated.

WORK

If you work for no money, but only to activate your card, every human being is treated and valued identically. 1 Corinthians 12 verse 7: "But the manifestation of the Spirit is given to each one for the profit of all." My definition of being rich is if you can comfortably provide yourself with shelter, food and clothing. The charity survival card system will make every human being rich. The largest unrecognized workforce on Earth throughout the history of humankind, mothers, will receive card activation upon the birth of their first baby. We will eliminate unemployment and poverty by beginning to provide shelter, food, water, sanitation and clothing to every human being worldwide, requiring they become employed to activate their charity survival card. Survival assessment teams will assess the world to develop plans to construct and or provide any such required infrastructures. Local people will always be included in the construction of such required infrastructures. They will also receive full hands-on training of operation and maintenance. Any required maintenance equipment will be provided on an ongoing basis.

BENEFITS

Working fathers will receive substantial paternity benefits regardless of employer. Sick leave will be available to everyone, regardless of employer. Retirement benefits will be provided to every working human being. Retirement is possible with the accumulation of 52,000 hours. I calculated this with a starting working age of twenty-five years old, working 2,080 hours per year and retiring at age fifty. Numbers 8 verses 24 and 25 24 "This is what pertains to the Levites: From twenty-five years old and above one may enter to perform service in the work of the tabernacle of meeting; and at the age of fifty years they must cease performing this work, and shall work no more."

This will eliminate any worries, anxiety and stress, of being required to work for a single company with a retirement benefit plan sufficient to provide enough to retire on and invest money into RRSPs or the like. Sick day benefits will be tracked together with employment hours by scanning in and out of the doctor's office for appointments. The cards would use biometrics to uniquely identify the in hand holder as the owner of the card before it is active to be used. Three weeks will be given for vacation regardless of employer. Health, vision and dental insurance will be eliminated because such services will be provided to anyone with an activated card. Without the money barrier, orphanages can be built and staffed to properly provide service worldwide.

The card would become the standard business security card. It would not require a PIN, because of biometric identification as mentioned above. Access to secure work areas or locked equipment storage could be controlled by card access. Each work day will be time recorded. This will accumulate every hour worked from your first day, regardless of the companies worked for. This is the way that the Canadian CPP and OAS will not be required. With an activated card, you will be able to obtain and do everything required for survival and communications worldwide. Survival is free. Policies and procedures would be put in place to deter misuse, abuse and work performed contributes to the survival of humankind. Parents will provide their children with survival requirements until the age of maturity.

EDUCATION

Students in post-secondary education will receive card activation. Without the financial barrier, the majority of people will complete their post-secondary education to perform their desired and chosen career. All education institutions will immediately increase in size to accommodate the incredible increase in attendance.

COMMUNICATION

A standard global cellular system will be developed to simplify global communications. The Internet would be extended to every point on Earth, requiring the survival card system. We must refrain from letting personal material possessions keep us in captivity of Satan's deception of love for the human body, and personal material possessions resulting in worries, anxiety, lust stress, and fear. Consider Mark 9 verse 35: "And He sat down, called the twelve, and said to them, "If anyone desires to be first, he shall be last of all and servant of all."

If we choose to use the charity survival card system, every human being will be working as a servant of all. After all, we will all work for the survival of humankind, not for your own personal gain above anyone else. Luke 10 verse 7: "And remain in the same house, eating and drinking such things as they give, for the laborer is worthy of his wages. Do not go from house to house." Because all of us are the laborers, we all deserve our wages, which is all we will require to survive.

We also seek and desire a life free of pollution. The system eliminates the need to be better than anyone else by getting a better paying job. The worry, anxiety and stress of not receiving a yearly raise are eliminated. The requirements for life will change, and this will relieve many worries, anxieties and stressors. People will remain working at jobs they are qualified for and love doing. If you love your job, you will never work a day in your life!

With an activated card, all hospital, medical and prescription drugs are available. This eliminates the worries, anxiety and stress of not being able to afford healthcare worldwide. With a free activated life card, once we convert to the charity survival card system, which is a world free of money, businesses will increase staff, as work requires. Those human beings unfortunate to not have a job on conversion to the charity survival card system will easily be provided with employment. Without financial barriers, it will be easy to provide sufficient food to those who are starving in under-developed countries until self-sufficiency is achieved.

Repairing the devastation pollution has done to the Earth and making it nearly nonlife-sustaining will be next. With no need to sell anything, businesses will not choose to cut corners on safety, functionality, or features. They will have adequate staff to eliminate employees overworking hours to ensure the product is profitable. A money-free world will eliminate the occurrence of layoffs because of tough financial times for a business. Where would the worries, anxiety and stress of inflation be in a money-free world? The taxes will be eliminated worldwide.

The use of sex in advertisements will be eliminated, along with every form of pornography to reduce the obsession and fascination humankind has for the visible physical human body. This obsession often results in jealousy, lust, envy, covetousness, fornication, adultery, lying and murder (abortion). Humankind must eliminate fornication. Humankind must revert to the true meaning of marriage, being the "I do" to sexual intercourse. This will enable humankind to focus on the invisible heart, spirit and mind of human beings that only requires the visible physical body to survive on Earth. Regardless of all else that occurs, with the deep physical attraction between male and female human beings, there is the possibility of procreation to ensure the human species does not go extinct, which is the same instinct that every living creature on Earth has. This will greatly increase the formation of true giving from your heart love relationships, which will result in stable loving families.

This free world would be best accomplished by a perfectly planned, big bang implementation. Of course, with such a cataclysmic change, there will be massive growing pains, but these must be accepted patiently and lovingly, and worked through to a resolution. Humankind will become one big happy family with no individual being of any more importance than another. Without the barrier of money, disaster relief and assistance will be more rapidly deployed with complete equipment to perform the work required to save lives. Natural disasters should be the only thing we need to save lives from. Any human activities possible to cause disaster would cease immediately; any manufacturing generating pollution and products used that generate pollution will cease immediately.

The next incredible challenge will be to increase the capacity of everything to accommodate items for free. Nevertheless, no increase in size will ever accommodate free attendance, but only increase in events to attend or accept to watch via television for free; there'll be no cost for anything except for individual's would be required to activate their charity survival card.

Any human being with an idea for a business or product could easily begin one because there is no requirement of being profitable to cover money costs of raw materials, workforce and benefits, marketing, logistics and point of sale. Products, accessibility and services will easily and rapidly be upgraded and or enhanced to accommodate people with disabilities. Standard guidelines of requirements of work to receive card activation will be accessible by every human being. One incredible new workforce will be card activation centers, which will provide card activation equipment to businesses that meet the standard requirements of contributing to the survival of humankind. There would be no need to be short of manufacturing any products required for survival.

The opposition I foresee to such a system would be those individuals who have had the privilege of acquiring more money than they could possibly ever use for just their survival. They refuse to accept the truth that the only thing all the money has brought into their lives is worries, anxiety, stress and fear; that someone else might do something to steal some of their money, or harm them or their children for some of their money or personal possessions. They hire such extensive personal guards and install such extensive alarm systems they might as well live in a prison. That does not sound like a life of complete joy and happiness to me, but each to their own. I do not suggest such a system for my own long-term benefit to survive, because I have more than enough money sources until I will be more than old enough; but only for those in this world who do not have less than enough to survive until tomorrow.

I am unable to think of a reason for discrimination of any kind using the charity survival card system. However, I have no experience discriminating, so it is difficult to understand what motivates it. I stand corrected! I discriminate against the filthy rich in this world who do nothing for those who are barely surviving. I choose not to be on the filthy rich side of life, because I am content owning only my computer, which is more than I require to survive. However, it is much more than anything else I require to survive, because I use it to have my daily devotional readings and man does not live by bread alone, but by every word from the mouth of God! I developed the Christ's on demand daily devotional readings in both audio and text formats, because of my extreme difficulty reading now being half blind! I wrote my thoughts of the charity survival card system months ago.

Something bothered me about the problems that could arise if a card is lost or stolen. There is technology available today that could be utilized to eliminate both of these possible problems, but with any technology there is the possibility of some type of problem or another. Businesses could provide their employees with an RFID microchip that would identify the employee and the business worked for. To eliminate the possible problems of losing it, or having it stolen, the microchip could be surgically implanted in the body. The problems with this are an employee might be fired or go to work for another company. However, this would easily be resolved by the microchip only containing a unique Personal identification number that businesses would use to select the person scanned information from a central database. There are so many other positive possible uses of RFID identification system. Houses could be modified to unlock the door hands free, with backup keyed entry if required. A person with difficult medical conditions could volunteer that their doctor update the central database with required relevant medical information that hospitals or paramedics could access in emergency situations.

TRANSPORTATION

There must be a complete change or conversion of our transportation to being pollution-free as soon as possible. This will require an exponential increase in employment worldwide. This will be the largest mega-construction project ever imagined since the creation of humankind. I envision a free electronic monorail rapid transit system worldwide. The result will be zero use of fossil fuels for transportation. This would require complete conversion of our infra-structures. With complete financial freedom from money, there would be no reason for delays due to cost or any such concern. Only the timeline to design, test, develop and construct. I'm sure it would be nearly impossible to esti-mate a timeline for such a project. With no financial barriers to overcome for anything on Earth, the size of constructing anything will never be a concern. However, without the money barriers required to overcome with today's projects, this timeline would be exponentially diminished. Furthermore, this system would eliminate the worries, anxiety and stress of our children learn-ing to drive and the outrageous number of deaths worldwide from automobile accidents.

Conversion would be to every house level. Every human being will have a chair to use in the system. There would be fold-out tables in the armrests, the seats would be heated with a heated floor pad in front of the chair. A glass bubble would enclose the chair for inclement weather. The chair will be used from the home to the mass rapid transit line. The chair will lock in place in the mass unit of the main line. Computers would be used to book you from point of origin to destination. This will determine your departure time from home, position in mass unit and arrival time at your destination. You would be able to pre-schedule recurring daily trips, such as to and from work for extended periods. This will enable the computer scheduler to best optimize the system. Airplanes would be converted to load and unload the chairs and to using hydrogen fuel. The main monorail lines would be through and between cities per continent. Reclining backs and extending footrests would be con-trolled by space limitations. Each chair would include a luggage compartment, which could not be opened while moving. Chair parking at public destinations would be used to encourage some physical activity.

Long-haul mass transit units could utilize tri-levels for increased capacity. However, this would increase safety complications of using washrooms in transit. Extensive research and design could possibly include washroom functionality per chair with dispensing waste at home. Adjustable gray scale functionality will be built into the glass bubble for privacy; numerous variations of privacy control could be used. Chair bubbles would need to adjust to bed position, including fully reclined back and footrest extended while sleeping for safety and comfort on long-haul trips. For safety reasons, the chair could not be set to bed position in single transit to mass transit units. A seatbelt would also be required and done up before the chair would become mobile. A flashing light will identify any chair seatbelt that is undone when locked into a mass unit. If the occupant refuses to refasten their seatbelt, within seconds an automated seatbelt would connect to ensure the mass unit is not delayed for departure.

The armrests would prevent occupant from rolling out of their chair in a bed position. Two seat chairs would be available for parent with child. Family units would require extensive detailed research and design. Trains and semi-trailers would need to be converted to burning hydrogen. Emergency vehicles will be converted to either electric or hydrogen power, or they could use a combination of both. With the removal of personal use vehicles from current roadways, the use of hydrogen should be safer.

I would like to see a standard cookie-cutter hospital designed with a complete training system to be able to build in any location requiring a hospital worldwide. If every human being lived lives of such love, no one would do anything that could possibly cause them any harm now or in the life to come! Because of this, the current impossibly unjust penal justice system could be eliminated and replaced with an equally impossibly just one.

LOVE JUSTICE SYSTEM

The "love justice system" means acceptance, confession, repentance and enough love for forgiveness to make the person who committed the crime not become a repeat offender. 1 Corinthians 6:7 Now therefore, it is already an utter failure for you that you go to law against one another. Why do you not rather accept wrong? Why do you not rather let yourselves be defrauded? If the person accused confesses to the person accusing them and asks for forgiveness, the person accusing them must forgive the person; or if they insist the person must be incarcerated, they are accepting responsibility to visit the person in prison to care for their well-being. Matthew 25 verse 36: "I was naked and you clothed Me; I was sick and you visited Me; I was in prison and you came to Me." Matthew 18 verses 21 and 22: 21 "Then Peter came to Him and said, 'Lord, how often shall my brother sin against me, and I forgive him? Up to seven times?"

22 Jesus said to him, 'I do not say to you, up to seven times, but up to seventy times seven.'"

The best judge for this justice system would be a lie detector. The accuser will ask only questions that can be answered with yes or no. Matthew 5 verse 37: "But let your 'Yes' be 'Yes,' and your 'No,' 'No.'" For whatever is more than these is from the evil one. If the person accused lies, they are accepting going to jail with no one required to visit them for their care and well-being. The only crime unforgivable by humankind is murder, because the person the murderer requires forgiveness from is dead! It is impossible for humankind to have any kind of a truly just justice system, because we never know perfectly what happened during the crime. Because of this, the impossibly just love justice system is more acceptable, because by using this we would learn the true purpose of the intense feeling of anger is to be sure you are aware of the amount of love required to resolve the reason for your anger.

Oh the joy life would be to know your work every day contributes to the survival of all humankind, not just your own. If you have experienced the true joy and happiness from giving from your heart true love relationship, you will want the life of joy and happiness of this singular joy and happiness multiplied by six billion human beings worldwide, for everyone is your neighbor! You will not be able to work as much as you want to, to have the continuous joy and happiness you will receive in your heart, soul and mind from true giving from your heart love for your neighbor; it will just keep you going wanting more joy and happiness. I pray that this life will be the first so-called virus that every human being will want to be infected with. I am confident it will, because there is nothing more powerful than love. The greater the love, the more powerful it is. For example, God is love and there is no being more powerful than God. I cannot think of a more peaceful, free and loving perfect world for humankind to live in. Not only does our subconscious mind want our conscious mind's thinking to be correct, but also we must think big to achieve big results, only the universe is bigger than the world.

I think the world is big enough for humankind to think about. Let us fix the Earth we have destroyed before we think about destroying another planet in the universe, and use all the time and effort seeking another planet to find ways to fix the Earth. Let us stop worrying about how much money we will need to build or fix something and worry about the amount of work we need to do to build or fix something. It is a sad state of affairs if humankind cannot decide to remove the one real barrier, money, from our freedom worldwide. Money stops us from providing the timely response required to save lives in natural disasters. Let's remove this death sentence on humankind! The list of pros of eliminating money is endless, but I am unable to think of a single con. Everyone is equal, there is no rich and poor, just rich. Everyone will be joyful and happy, content. The only real difference will be bosses, managers, workers and children. I guess that power generation could convert from building massive, environment-destroying generating stations into numerous smaller generating stations with relatively no environmental impact. I can only guess, but those in the know of every business worldwide would instantly know the pros for their business without a money barrier to worry about.

I am confident that with modern technology, this system would not be too difficult for the techno geniuses to develop. They only need the request from humankind to begin. Oh, if humankind would agree, this would be a perfect world; we could soon begin making it our reality! What humankind needs are leaders with the desire to provide the citizens of their countries with such a perfect world. The challenge is to gather them all together for a meeting to discuss the possibilities. It covers all aspects of world's dilemmas being discussed often by NGOs; there could be worldwide peace and security, agriculture, aquaculture and forestry, children, youth and family welfare, community development, disability issues, disasters and humanitarian affairs. We could implement worldwide education and training, energy, environment and climate change, financial accessibility and management. Everything from food security and nutrition, gender issues, HIV/AIDS, TB, malaria, health and medical, (resolved by cookie-cutter hospitals worldwide) could be addressed. This worldwide program would cover everything from human rights, information and communications, job creation and enterprise development, labour conditions, migration and population, refugees and internally displaced persons, shelter, housing, land management and construction, tourism, travel, leisure and sports, trade and development, transportation and logistics and water and related ecosystems.

With no financial barriers, every one of these global concerns will be easily addressed. The plan already has specific steps for many of these identified areas requiring resolutions. It is a universal amount of labor and effort; but without the financial barrier, it is possible to achieve resolutions to these outstanding global dilemmas we have caused here on Earth. We have caused this devastation to the Earth so we must do everything possible to correct them immediately. We are the generation that is required to begin repairing the Earth before it is too late. The Earth does not have much time left before Satan accomplishes his goal of making humankind make it non-life sustaining to make every living creature extinct worldwide. To be sure, humankind is prepared for this catastrophe, I say let's become the army of God (church of God) now as the body of Jesus Christ to be sure we all have everlasting life! We must not procrastinate on this; the beginning of the perfect life that will enable humankind to choose to work towards the perfect world. Satan has deceived humankind long enough. We only need to choose to take control of the perfect world God created for us to live on and as, lives of complete joy and happiness, lives of complete giving from your heart love. We need to have a love for God and for each other as yourself.

CHURCH

I will start by discussing the negative affect money has had on the church, which has combined with the attitude that we want everything to be easy. There are not sufficient hymns to have one related to every chapter of the Bible and it costs a lot of money to print and distribute hymnals, and I understand that these publishing companies need to preserve their livelihood. The word of God has more or less been put to death by the church setting a fixed calendar with a reading scheduled for each Sunday of the year. These are only from the chapters of the Bible that have a hymn related to them. This pre-concluded meaning of the messages in the Bible means it cannot lead the church through its life. Furthermore, the ELCIC has forsaken the laws of God to follow the laws of the land by passing a motion that same sex marriages will be blessed by the church! If same sex couples want to gain the financial benefits provided by the government by being married, they should go to a Justice of the Peace instead.

I would like to see a team organized to relate a hymn to every chapter of the Bible regardless of the denominational hymnals used. In addition each of these hymns, there should be music recorded on the piano. If we were free from money, the church calendar could be eliminated and weekly services could have the message provided by Jesus Christ through a web application like Christ's On-Demand Weekly Worship Service that has the related hymn text included at the end of each passage and an html5 audio player for the recorded piano music. The Bishop of the ELCIC had the perfect format for this kind of message. She would simply read the passage of scripture and ask each person present to talk about what the message meant to them. This would revitalize the Christian church and put Jesus Christ back at its head. Epiphany Lutheran Church has set a good example of how a rich suburban church can unite with a downtown, lower income area church like LUM to assist those in need to survive and flourish.

RECREATION

All children will have equal opportunities to participate in any organized sport they desire. People with the abilities to coach or referee organized sports will receive card activation, if they are consistent and chosen to continue with the team or sport.

CHAPTER SEVEN

Handling Change

Keep an open and positive mind. Look for the negatives you have lost or left behind. Look for the positives you have gained from the change; simply put, the negatives lost or left behind are the greatest positive of it all. I learned on January 16, 2006, by taking an on-line IQ test that I would probably be great at living with changes. In addition, I learn new things well and quickly. Here are some details from my IQ test. I believe this is most accurate in describing me.

> *Your Intellectual Type is: You have the unusual talent of being equally good at both mathematical and verbal skills. That, paired with your thirst to learn through experience, makes you an inventive inquisitor. Your strength lies in the methodology you have naturally adopted to understand the world. Basically, you have perfected "learning through living." You have a unique ability to teach others by taking them through actual experiences. Your talents come in handy, especially when confronted with unfamiliar or unproven situations. Most people search their brains for previously stored information that might help in a given situation. You, however, take things as they come and see*

things as they are. You are a great improviser and are probably open to an unusual amount of change.

Job 5 verse 17 Behold happy is the man whom God corrects; Therefore do not despise the chastening of the Almighty. I think the perfect example of my intellect is the following: On November 22 2013 I attended a multicultural communication session at work. It involved playing a card game in which not a word could be spoken. I was unable to read the one page of instructions before the game started. I was only able to play, because the instructor I knew agreed to hold my hand of cards for me. There were no face cards in the deck used. The winner of the game would move one table clockwise. Thank God, I was dealt a very good hand for the rules of this table that I learned spades were trump on the first hand played. I used my extensive experience playing Kaiser while working for Petro Canada to know how to take the most tricks possible with a trump suit. I managed to short suit myself in two suits relatively quickly to be able to use my low trump cards to take tricks. I won the first game, taking five tricks moving one table clockwise. Another player tried to use a club as trump on the first hand and a paper was quickly written to pass around, no trump! I did not have a no trump hand and did not take one trick in the second game.

I write this by my experience, how I have managed to handle all the changes in my life since 2002, when I became a half physically dead miracle man walking. I feel I must explain my wording. The majority of the right side of my brain was damaged from four bleeds in my brain due to burst aneurysms in December 2002. I lost the sense of touch on the entire left side of my body, but thank God for the blessing of still feeling pain on the entire left side of my body. Without the sense of pain, I would have no idea if something happened that required my attention. I also lost the entire left side of my field of vision.

How to handle losing positives in the change: for you may lose positives as well as negatives, which needs to be accepted to be able to enable yourself to move on and do the best you can with whatever is left. You must not concentrate only on one of the types of changes, but be sure to be aware of both types of changes to avoid allowing either type to become more negative, which is a great challenge for me. I also lost my sense of awareness, or recognition, making it impossible for me to be aware of anything now. One of the strangest inconvenience, or the most annoying change that occurred in my life since miraculously surviving four massive hemorrhagic strokes, is my nose runs continuously. This has made me conclude the reason colds are the most common incurable sickness most human beings suffer from. It's the normal way a human body must function to keep the parts of the body lubricated as required; but one congests it by the negative thinking that you are sick if your nose begins to run uncontrollably. I do not think I have a cold, I just blow my nose as required to be presentable in public. However, this was most extreme on August 22, 2013, when I used an entire box of Kleenex blowing my nose in one day! I continued my stair climbing exercises this entire day as well, with only my first run being the slowest timed since July 26, 2013: 37.78 seconds. My last run of the day was only 34.06 seconds, only .06 slower than my personal record of 34.00 seconds!

The greatest change in my life was being forced to accept the truth that I require asking people to help me do almost everything in my life physically now opposed to me helping other people physically. I know from experience that I am high in depression, so I do not let my thoughts dwell on everything

I am not able to do now physically; but I concentrate on what I am able to do now, or how or what I might need to change to do the most I am able to do. I've learned not to worry about what others might think of me in determining how to do things. I must do anything now while living half physically dead and being a miracle man walking! Ignorance is Bliss I now have complete trust in God, combined with giving from my heart love for my neighbor as myself, which is the perfect life. It is a life of complete joy and happiness; a life free of worry, anxiety, stress and fear. Humankind seeks desires and we are required to be living now at the end of the age. I can honestly say that living without the sense of awareness is blissful. You must take positive action to handle any negative changes that you are able to change yourself. Do not worry or dwell on any changes that you can do nothing to change for the positive and trust

God will give you the wisdom to know the difference, but accept it and move forward, doing the best you are able due to the change. Such as the normal way for a human body to react if there is a loss of brain control, which is to contract inward to try the utmost to protect vital organs. My left foot is constantly contracted or rotated inward, resulting in the outside left of the toe of my left foot dragging as I step forward. Without the sense of touch, and or awareness, I have no idea this is happening to even try to straighten it out.

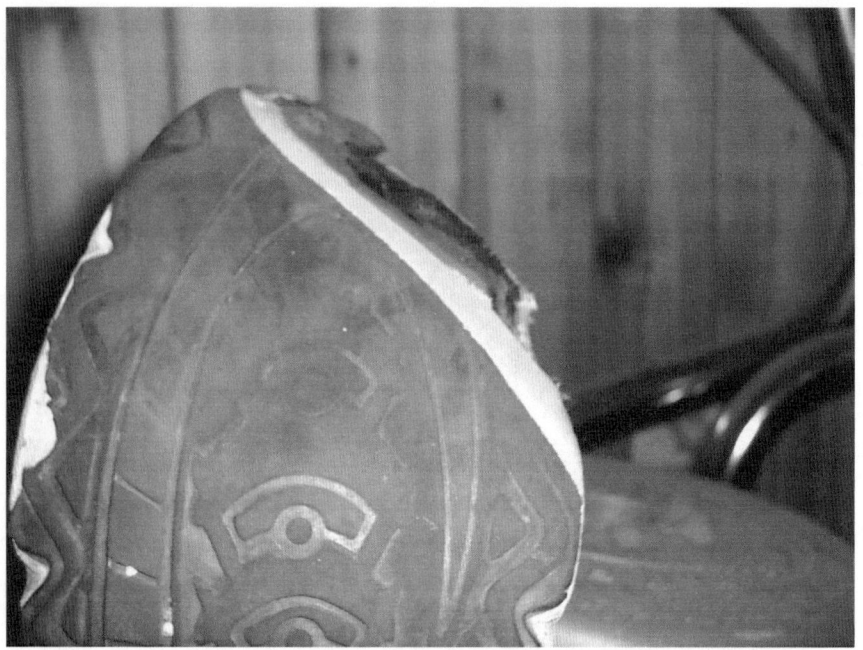

Here's a view from bottom of hole worn in my left shoe!
(key this into the command line of your browser to view the
image on-line! www.keithlistoe.ca/S2020321.JPG)

Here's another bottom view of the hole worn in my left shoe.
(key this into the command line of your browser to view the
image on-line! www.keithlistoe.ca/S2020322.JPG)

I am only able to straighten it if I look at my foot to watch it as I take a step, but it is a hazard enough for me walking, being half blind now. Thank God my son, Cody, is a welder and successfully made the Keith's less toe protecting footwear, 3/16-stainless steel-toe cover for me, and the shoe guy at the Grant Park Shopping Center put Velcro straps on it to hold it on my footwear.

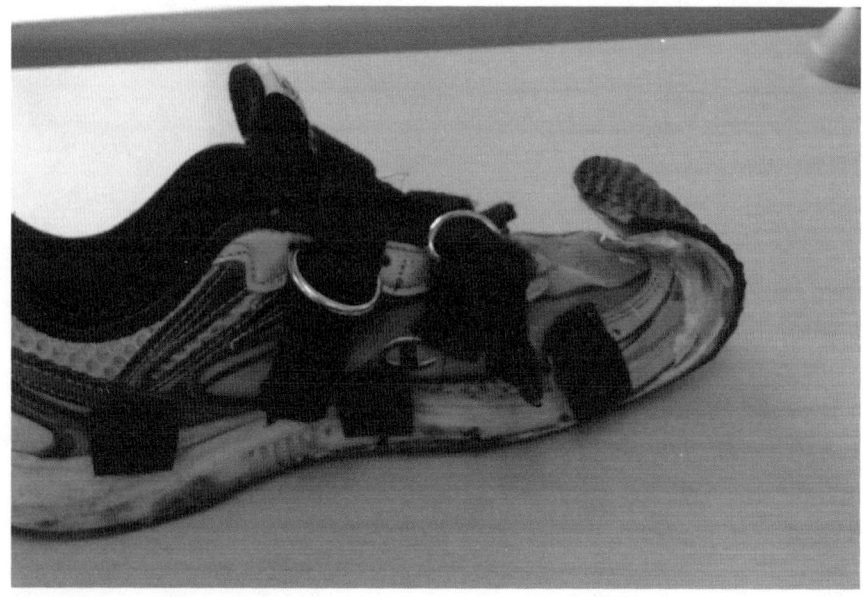

Here's my Keith's less toe-protecting footwear 3/16 stainless steel toe cover.
(key this into the command line of your browser to view the image on-line!
www.keithlistoe.ca/Keithlesstoe_protecting_footwear_steel_toe_cover.jpg)

The picture included is the third version as a permanent attachment to my footwear now to avoid the straps coming undone and the Keith's less toe-protecting footwear flying off my foot and swinging into my right foot, which hurt it greatly once. The original prototype is now used as a special peddle on my adult tricycle, enabling me to ride it without worrying that my left foot will fall off the pedal without me knowing it until I feel the pain of riding over it or such.

Prototype converted to special pedal on my adult tricycle!
(key this into the command line of your browser to view the
image on-line! www.keithlistoe.ca/special_pedal.jpg)

I am more comfortable riding my tricycle than walking, because I can turn my head to the left to be sure I see more without losing my balance as I do if I turn my head too far as I'm walking. I also wear a bright reflective vest now if I go outside for a walk or to ride my tricycle anywhere, after I was struck by a small red car on May 24, 2012. That happened as I was walking across Main Street at Broadway, late in the evening after dark. I was wearing my dark blue spring jacket, making it nearly impossible for the young woman driving to see me before I was on the hood of her car. This is also when I thought, 'I am on the hood of the car; I can hear the brakes screeching'. It happened so fast from my blind left side, while I was returning home from the St. Vital Mall. I was preparing to ride my tricycle to the Petro Canada Lubricants Warehouse on Friday, May 25, 2012, to go to Saskatoon, Sk with it on Sunday, May 27, 2012

On my adult tricycle with my reflective vest in Spiritwood, Sk. in 2012!
(key this into the command line of your browser to view the
image on-line! www.keithlistoe.ca/Keith_on_trike.jpg)

My son, Tyler, has installed turn signals, switches and lights on my tricycle, along with a brake light operated by my hand brake. I have also asked him to research converting a power wheelchair to include a gasoline engine battery charger, which will greatly increase the range I could travel with it at a maximum speed of five miles per hour. I was able to have this idea because Tyler was a member of the SAE University of Manitoba team that built a hybrid Formula One race car and he has graduated as an electrical engineer now.

I have often experienced the strange ability to understand a question, even though the person they were asking did not understand it. I was able to reword the question for them to understand and answer it. My work experiences proved I learn new things quickly and well per the following: I had to find a job in Saskatoon, Saskatchewan, in September/October of 1981. My Uncle John, living in Saskatoon, was also looking for work. He was tired of getting laid off every winter, and then being called back to work in the spring. He was working for the city of Saskatoon Parks and Recreation Department then. He phoned me one Thursday afternoon with a request that I go take his interview for a job the next day that he didn't want. The job did not pay as much as he was getting from unemployment insurance, so I phoned the company doing the interview to ask if it was okay that I came instead of my Uncle John, and they said sure. I met with Garry Paulson, the owner and founder of the company, Startco Engineering, on Friday morning. At the end of the interview, he asked me if I was available to start work on Monday and I said yes. I was hired!

The work was electrical assembly of large power centers used by the potash industry to control supply power to the large electric motors used in the mines. Learning how to assemble these machines was all on the job training. After two weeks of training, Bill Landman, the supervisor, said I was ready to work on my own, which I was successful at doing.

Keith in front of mining machine in the Lanigan Potash mine!
(key this into the command line of your browser to view the image
on-line! www.keithlistoe.ca/Keith_in_front_of_potash_miner.jpg)

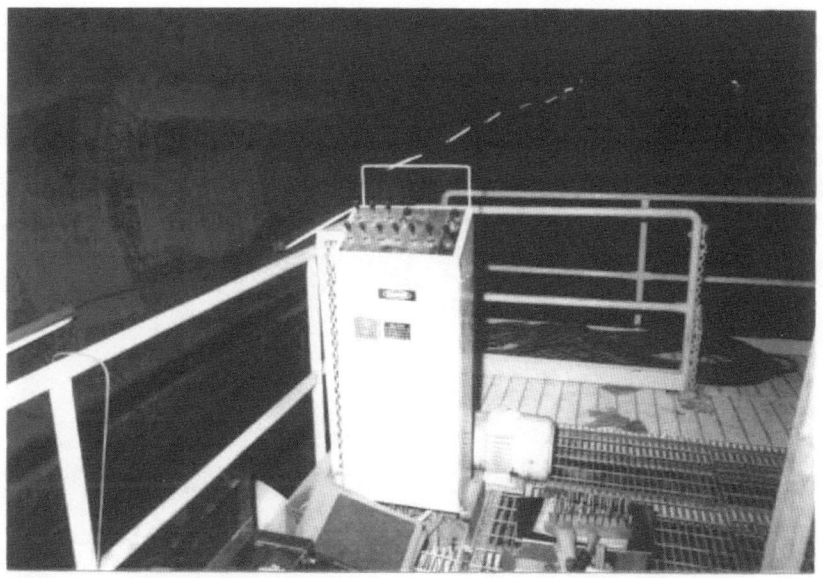

Here's a roof bolter and overhead crane control pedestal I installed on the mining
machine in the Lanigan Potash mine!
(key this into the command line of your browser to view the image on-line!
www.keithlistoe.ca/overhead_crane-roof_bolter_control_console_I_designed_built-inst.jpg)

Here's a picture of assembling the roof bolter and overhead crane
control pedestal in the shop!
(key this into the command line of your browser to view the image on-line!
www.keithlistoe.ca/startco_my_crane-roof_bolter_pedestal_interior.jpg)

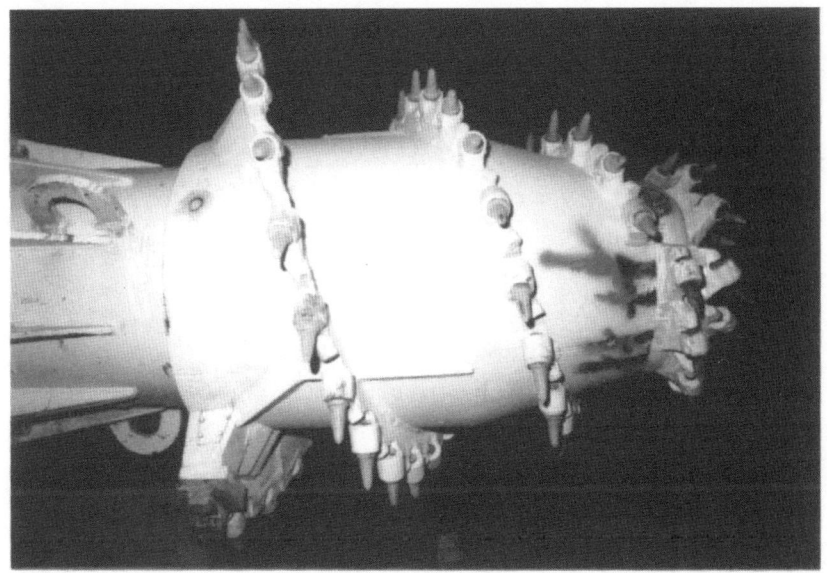

Here's a close-up of the new overhead rotating booms added to
the base Marietta mining machine!
(key this into the command line of your browser to view the image on-line!
www.keithlistoe.ca/potash_miner_New_overhead_rotating_booms_closeup.jpg)

Here's the engineer who designed the installed control console for the new overhead rotating booms.
(key this into the command line of your browser to view the image on-line!
www.keithlistoe.ca/potash_miner_New_control_centre.jpg)

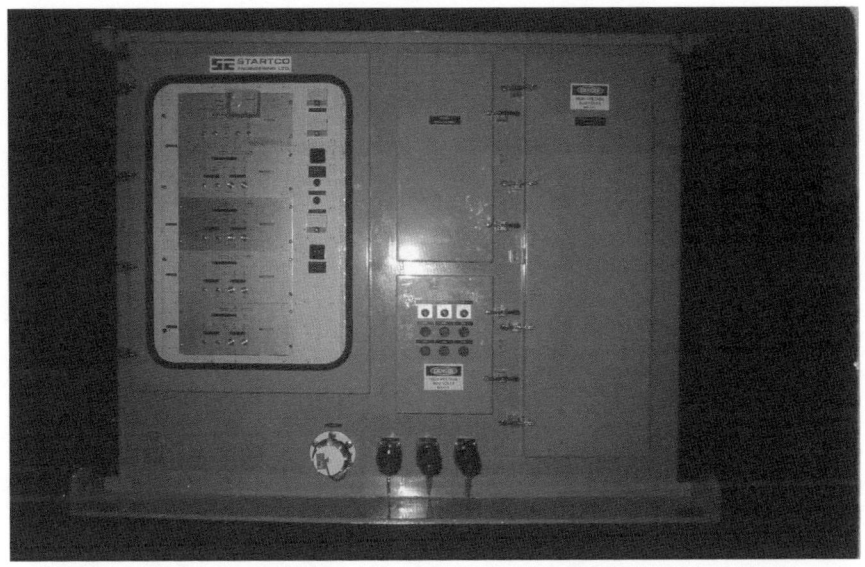

This is the end of the Luscar power center.
(key this into the command line of your browser to view the image
on-line! www.keithlistoe.ca/startco_luscar_power_centre.jpg)

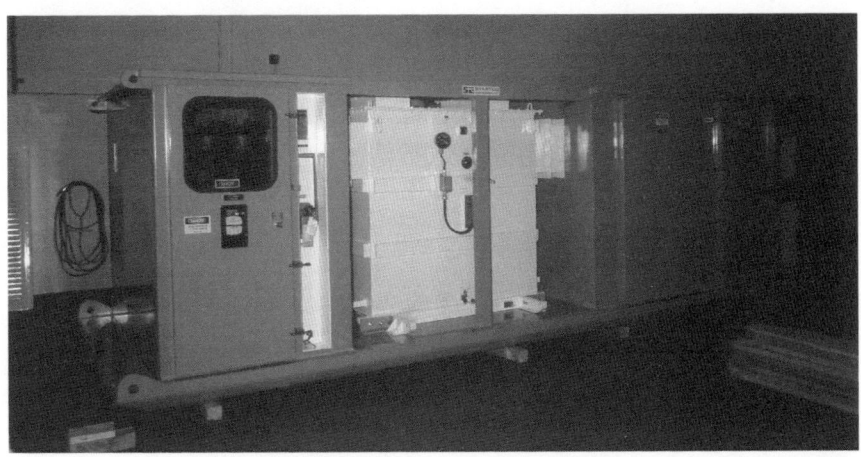

This is a side of Luscar power center!
(key this into the command line of your browser to view the image
on-line! www.keithlistoe.ca/startco_luscar_power_centre2.jpg)

Here is the loading of the completed Luscar power center on a flat-bed trailer for delivery to the customer!
(key this into the command line of your browser to view the image on-line! www.keithlistoe.ca/startco_luscar_power_centre3.jpg)

I was told that this was the quickest anyone had been allowed to work on their own! After a couple months, they introduced a bonus plan to increase the best worker's pay. This went as follows: Bill allotted so many hours to complete each machine. Each employee would time stamp in and out for the total number of hours worked on it. If the machine was completed in fewer hours than allotted, the difference in hours would be added to the bonus pot. At the end of the month, the supervisor, divided the bonus pot by the number of employees plus one. Each employee's time was analyzed to determine who had contributed the most hours to the pot. This employee would receive the extra portion of the bonus pot. I received this extra bonus pay for six consecutive months. My co-workers were not very happy, as they could not work faster than I could, even though they had been working there for two or three years and I wasn't even there a year yet.

I was successful in getting a job with Northern Telecom in their electronics assembly division, where they assembled the electronic equipment for transmitting and receiving information over the fiber optic cables they manufactured and sold. My pay rate at Startco was just over $5 per hour and my starting rate at NT was $9.25 per hour. When I went in to tell Garry Paulson that I was quitting, taking this better paying job, he asked, "How much are they offering?" I told him $9.25 per hour. He said, "I would match their pay if you stay here working for Startco. I also have plans to open another shop to assemble vibration controllers, which I was hoping you would operate for Startco." I had to refuse, as I believed there was more opportunity at NT, but when I went out to the back to say goodbye to my co-workers, I told them that Garry was offering over $9 per hour. They should all go talk to him. Garry was very mad at me for doing this as he gave them each this raise.

However, many years later, I talked to him and he was very grateful that I had done this. After that, he had very little turnover in his staff, which was a major problem before this.

NT seemed like a great company to work for. Again, I learned very quickly, my first job there being in first assembly. In the first six weeks working at NT, I had five different jobs, each one with an increase in pay. These jobs were first assembly, second assembly, quality inspection, supervisor – evening shift and tester two, almost doubling my starting wage in the process. As well as being able to work unlimited overtime. When I started working for NT, I was one of the six male employees in the plant. Because this equipment was all new technology, there were nothing off the shelf to do any of the testing, but the tests had to be developed. I worked directly with the engineers who designed the equipment to write the test procedures for the FD565 system test I was to perform on every board manufactured.

Shortly after I started working for Petro Canada in 1987, I had an idea of how to rearrange the product in the storage shelves to improve my efficiency in picking orders. The foreman, did not like my ideas, but Bill Soloway did, so he and I rearranged the products in the storage shelves. One day around 1988-1989, both Walter and Bill were off on the same day. I arrived at work seeing five boxcars on the south side of the warehouse. I knew I needed to pick the orders for the city deliveries first thing, then I would start unloading the first boxcar till mid-afternoon, when I knew I needed to begin picking the orders for out-of-town deliveries. I worked as fast and safely as I possibly could. Totally surprising myself, I unloaded and put away all five boxcars by mid-afternoon. Then I completed picking all the out-of-town orders. The next day, Walter and Bill asked me how many people I hired to help me unload five boxcars and pick all the orders. I replied, "None, without the two of you in my way slowing me down, I was able to work much faster and efficiently, completing it all safely with no problems or spills of any kind."

I still have photographic face recognition for any face I knew before 2002, but extremely limited for new faces I have seen since then. I thank God, because I do recognize all of the following listed people now:

Name	Work	Bowling	Church	Other	On the bus
1. unknown if I can use name	1				
2. Not allowed to use name	1				
3. Not allowed to use name	1				
4. Art Hilderman			1		
5. Audrey Hilderman			1		
6. Barbara Nixon	R				
7. Bernie Cope		1			
8. Betsy Ross	1				
9. Bill Antymniuk	X	1			
10. unknown if I can use name		1			
11. Bob Bartlette			1		
12. Bob Clow			1		

13. Brenda boards bus at Balmoral station					1
14. Not allowed to use name	1				
15. Brent Day			1		
16. Brian Wills	1				
17. Not allowed to use name	1				
18. Bob Wiebe	1				
19. Bud Filby			1		
20. Carlyle Safeway customer service				1	
21. Carol Cope		1			
22. Not allowed to use name	1				
23. unknown if I can use name		1			
24. Cindy Nachtigall			1		
25. Craeg Parker			1		
26. Not allowed to use name	1				
27. Chris Loeppky	1				
28. Colette Jamieson	1				
29. Dale Boyer			1		
30. Dan Prowse	1				
31. Darcy Pagan deceased March 31 2014			1		
32. Darrel Sunka		1			

33. David Meier	1				
34. Debbie Superstore teller				1	
35. Dolly Marbil	1				
36. Dorothy Pagan			1		
37. Doug Bradley		1			
38. Drew Deck			1		
39. Dwayne Muth			1		
40. Elaine Lochhead			1		
41. Eileen Clow			1		
42. Eldon Hemminger	1				
43. Erin Green	1				
44. Esther Weiss			1		
45. Farhana Jahan	1				
46. Fran Robinson		1			
47. Gail Anderson			1		
48. Not allowed to use name	1				
49. Garry Grant	X	1			
50. Gary Oake			1		
51. Gennaro Pellegrino	1				
52. Georg Schreckenbach			1		
53. Not allowed to use name	1				

54. Gerald Safeway manager				1	
55. Glen Reitmeier	1				
56. Guy Arbez	1				
57. Harold Weiss			1		
58. Ian Mann	1				
59. Ingthor Isfeld			1		
60. Jack Moore			1		
61. Jamie Hall	1		1		
62. Not allowed to use name	1				
63. Joey Dikkema			1		
64. Jodie Lowe	1				
65. John Hart	1				
66. John Ziesmann	1				
67. Jill Johnson	1				
68. Jolie Hrominchuk			1		
69. Judy Dikkema			1		
70. Judy Grant	X	1			
71. June Day			1		
72. Karie Moroz			1		
73. Katherine Bartmanovich			1		
74. Katherine Thorstienson			1		

75. Keith Shaw departs bus at Main at Broadway					1
76. Keith Single			1		
77. Kelly Crone			1		
78. Kim Andre	1				
79. Not allowed to use name	1				
80. Kris Nelson	1				
81. Not allowed to use name	1				
82. Larry Chaput	1				
83. Lauro Pagtakhan	1				
84. Lawrence security guard Manitoba Hydro	1				
85. Lily Geltke			1		
86. Linda - boarded the bus at Lakeside					1
87. Lisa Legge	1				
88. Lois Chancellor square apartments				1	
89. Lynne Gauthier	1				
90. Malony Capina	1				
91. Mark Mandzik	1				
92. Mark Olfert		1			
93. Marilyn Bradley		1			
94. Maureen Monson			1		

95. Mekdes boards bus at Ellice @ Edmonton					1
96. Michael Manitoba Hydro Place	1				1
97. Michaela Browning	1				
98. unknown if I can use name	1				
99. Mona Hiebert	1				
100. Monica Deck			1		
101. unknown if I can use name	1				
102. Netty					1
103. Nick Hrominchuk			1		
104. Nicole Wingate	1				
105. Peter Knip			1		
106. Paul Baker	1				
107. Paul Bergsagel			1		
108. Paul Funk	X				
109. Paul Pattyn	1				
110. Paul Safeway customer service				1	
111. Paul Straszynski	1				
112. Peter Buscemi	1				

113. Peter Roth	1				
114. Phil Enns			1		
115. Rene Roy	1				1
116. Rick Walker	X	1			
117. Not allowed to use name	1				
118. Rob Monson			1		
119. Robert Boni	1				
120. Roger Rosenberg			1		
121. Rolando Banilbo boards bus at Balmoral Station					1
122. Ron Monson			1		
123. Rory security guard Manitoba Hydro Place	1				
124. Ryan Armstrong	1				
125. Ryan Kitz	1				
126. Sandy Safeway customer service				1	
127. Shirley Knip			1		
128. Steve Reimer	1				
129. Steve security guard Manitoba Hydro Place	1				

130. Not allowed to use name	1				
131. Taomi-Safeway customer service				1	
132. Terri Keith	1				
133. Terry Liu	1				
134. Trevor Sinclair	1				
135. Tyler Pajak mail room Manitoba Hydro Place	1				
136. unknown name boards bus at Carlton going home	1				
137. unknown name boards bus going home at Graham @ Fort wearing ear set plugs.					1
138. Unknown name on bus in front left side seat wearing blue Kentucky Wildcats baseball cap departs at Main and Broadway then boards going home at Pembina at Windermere					1
139. unknown name boards bus at Fort Rouge station departs at Portage @ Donald MTS Center					1

140. Vickie Albrecht			1		
141. Werner Toews	1				
142. Xueshan Geng	1				
143. Zach Regiec	1				
Name	**Work**	**Bowling**	**Church**	**Other**	**On the bus**
Total	68	13	44	7	11
					143

I'm even more thankful that I remember all of these new names now, because before the bleeds in my brain, as mentioned earlier, I had photographic new face recognition, but I could not remember any new names when I met someone. I have decided to try harder to remember names, because at least it is a person I do not recognize, I can ask and they can answer. I also do not recognize vehicles, but had to wait until I could read the license plate on my own 2002 Pontiac Grand Prix to know it was Teri coming to pick me up. I must consciously think about everything I look at now to recognize or know what I am seeing. Furthermore, since 2000, I have lost or unknowingly given away over $1 million in personal net worth. I had started my own SAP consulting business named LISTUEN Corp. on July 1, 1997, with a contract with Agreevo NA, under a subcontract through Tullamore Advantage, on a subcontract with Earnst and Young. I earned approximately $1.3 million in income over the first three years of business without any advertising or marketing, but I also spent $1.3 million in expenses. I had fourteen weeks paid vacation in the third year to enjoy all the toys I had bought with all the money, I had earned.

Me in front of my 1999 Z20 Mariah inboard boat!!!
(key this into the command line of your browser to view the
image on-line! www.keithlistoe.ca/myboat_new.jpg)

My 1999 28.5-foot Terry fifth wheel trailer!
(key this into the command line of your browser to view the image
on-line! www.keithlistoe.ca/traileroutside_slideout_side.jpg)

I made the mistake of letting my insurance lapse in 2002, so I had no disability insurance when I had the four massive hemorrhagic strokes in December 2002, resulting in me living off my outstanding work and personal credit lines. Through the assistance of my occupational therapist at the Health Sciences Center Hospital, I began receiving CPP disability insurance in the fall of 2003. I had no idea if I was still able to work like I did before, because everything was from my memory of how the SAP System could be configured and I did not have my own personal copy of it to try anything in.

I decided, to see if I could volunteer at Manitoba Hydro to determine if I was able to work like I did before, before I bid on any new jobs under my own business, LISTUEN Corp. The first test was I could not log onto the computer I was sitting at. I did my own problem solving after numerous failed attempts to log-on and I found the network cable was not plugged into the back of the computer. I plugged it in and had no problems logging on after that. I was able to provide suggestions after my first week as a volunteer to enable them to resolve one long outstanding problem. This provided me the confidence that I was still able to work like I did before the strokes.

Manitoba Hydro then asked me if I would like to try configuring the system for e-mail outputs of purchasing documents in a test system. I successfully completed this configuration through January and February of 2004. I received a phone call from a previously used third party in March of 2004 saying, "We have heard of everything that has happened to you, but Hercules wants to know if you are still able to work like you did before." I answered, "Yes, I am still able to work like I did before, but I am unable to drive now."

I thought, this is great; I will be able to make enough money to clear my debt. I phoned the manager, Charlie Carbo, I knew at Hercules to ask him what the reason for this call was. He answered, "We have had SAP working on our problems for the past two years and they only say it is impossible for the system to do what we need it to do; so we thought, our only chance of resolving these problems was if you are still able to work like you used to." I accepted this work for Hercules in Wilmington, Delaware, performing one week of work in Wilmington and a second week remotely from home. I resolved one problem completely, but the second only proved to them that the system could do what they needed it to do. They were unable to provide the logic to have me resolve the problem properly, though. However, through further enhancement development of the e-mail process at Manitoba Hydro, I heard for the first time working with the SAP Software, "this is perfect." The functionality developed is a new technique that would resolve Hercules's problem perfectly as well, but I no longer do any SAP consulting.

This new concept or technique makes the computer work for you and not you working for the computer; it's user friendly. In brief, this is to present the user with the information available to enable them to select the information they want to use, as opposed to having to manually search for it.

I had to pay my travel expenses upfront and bill the third party for them in addition with my billable hours. Hercules paid the third party promptly, but the third party never paid me. I became angrier and angrier when this man refused to even talk to me on the phone, but instantly hung up when he heard my voice. I became sickened with my thoughts of what I could, should and would do to make this man pay me without the hassle and expense of using lawyers. I only had to convince my logical thinking mind that I would be okay if I only reduce my standard of living to pay off my outstanding debt, which was now double what it was before doing this work for Hercules.

In June 2004, I received a request from Manitoba Hydro to take a paid position to cover an employee going off on maternity leave. I accepted this offer of employment and began on June 14, 2004, in the SAP Support Services Department at Manitoba Hydro. I received a number of temporary positions until August 31, 2006, when I received the news that Bob Brennan, the President and CEO, had personally approved me for a permanent position. Through my daily devotional readings in 2007, I made the decision to forgive the man who refused to pay me. I instantly received complete peace of heart, soul and mind!

In 1987, Petro Canada announced a program to help their employees purchase their own personal computers. I knew nothing about personal computers other than my cousin, Alan Listoe, had bought an Apple II+, so I phoned him to ask his advice on which of the two computers I should buy, being one with a 5.25-inch floppy disk drive or the second with a 20 MB hard drive. He recommended the computer with the 5.25-inch floppy disk drive. I ignored his advice and bought the IBM 286 with the 20 MB hard drive. The computer arrived at the supplying company on a Thursday, but they did not have anyone to deliver it before the weekend, so I asked if I could pick it up from the store.

When I turned it on, the menu on the screen was the name of the supplying company. I immediately decided '*I sure do not want that as the menu for my personal computer*'. I had received a DOS manual with the computer, so I thought it must be in there how to display information on the screen. By Sunday evening, the screen read 'the Listoe computer main menu', with all the same options the original menu had. On Monday morning, the supplying company phoned to ask if I would like a technician to come out to verify I had set everything up correctly. I thought, '*what harm it could do to have it professionally verified?*', so I agreed. A woman from this company arrived just after lunch on Monday. She called me into the room, asking me if there was a phone she could use. I brought her a phone and sat down beside her. She called the manager at her company, telling him, "The computer started with no problems, but the menu is the Listoe computer main menu and I have no idea what to do." I quickly interrupted her saying, "Thank you for coming over, but you may leave now!"

This was shortly after our first child was born that made my finances very tight, which did not enable me to spend any money on software, so I pirated software programs from whomever I could. However, this forced me to learn each program by myself without any printed documentation. I do remember that I had Lotus 123, Word Perfect and dbase II, but after I bought and installed Windows, I then bought and converted to Microsoft Office Suite of applications, especially Excel and Word. When the first SAP Instructor started learning how to use a mouse in March of 1992 on SAP R3 version 1.1, I immediately decided that I could learn the software quicker myself than watch her learn how to use a mouse; so I ignored her and learned the SAP software as I had learned all previous software on my personal computer.

We had a new instructor named Pascal Nass. Pascal was from Paris and was still learning to speak English, but he spoke well enough for me to realize he had an in-depth knowledge of the SAP system. After his first week he said, "Okay, I think we are ready to start configuring our own company in the system." I quickly responded, "I have already configured my own company in the system." He said, "Okay, I will use your company to show what we have not learned yet to make it usable." He created a customer, then a material code and received some inventory into the plant for his material. He then created a sales order to his customer for some material. He created the delivery note for the sales order, picked it and post goods issue for the delivery. He was completely shocked that there were no errors on the financial postings because he had not taught any of the configurations for it yet. I was only able to learn the SAP System so well and quickly because I was on the system learning it for about 16.5 hours per day. I could see and understand the benefits the SAP System would make for my day-to-day job in inventory management, so I was eager to put in the extra hours while on the road to simplify my job in the long run.

I lived on only four hours of sleep until the bleeds in my brain happened in December 2002! I never had any moments in my life that I felt tired or sleepy, regardless of the hours of sleep I had in a night. My first experience working on a computer is a great example of learning new things quickly and well. I was registered in the faculty of Engineering at the University of Saskatchewan in 1981; although I only had enough money to make a deposit on my tuition, thinking I would get a student loan. However, my student loan was rejected and I was told that if I did not pay my tuition within two days of classes, I would be kicked out and I would lose my deposit. I took two days of classes in the computer sciences class learning the FORTRAN IV programming language. I was unsuccessful in getting either of the two programming assignments to work, but after I was promoted to operations supervisor and relocated to Winnipeg, Mb. in 1991 working for Petro Canada.

The lubricants warehouse in Winnipeg had six large bulk oil storage tanks that had to be measured and temperature corrected to 15 degrees Celsius daily. To do so, a co-efficient was found in this 2-inch thick book for the temperature and viscosity of oil being converted. The FORTRAN program that was used to print all of the coefficients was printed at the end of this book. I had the idea that this whole process, which took over an hour each day, would be much more efficient if I could convert the FORTRAN program into an Excel function module and write a data entry macro for the readings each day. I was successful in this. The entire process was reduced to less than five minutes and I included an overview spreadsheet that kept track from day-to-day if there was a loss of oil to know for certain a leak was occurring.

Further positive changes in my life came from my daily devotional readings in 2007. I decided to donate the majority, 169 items, of my personal household possessions, except what I required to cook and serve a Christmas feast for five homeless people here in Winnipeg, which is also everything I required to survive. I had to be thankful when only one of the people I invited actually came over for the Christmas feast, because I did not cook even enough food for her and my three children present to eat with me. I did not have more than one bite of turkey for my Christmas dinner in 2007, but I was okay. I did not need any more than this to survive. I finally managed to sell my one remaining possession of any value, my 28.5-foot Terry fifth wheel trailer, in October 2008, which enabled me to buy Christmas dinner feast for all of the people supported by Siloam Mission;

This was my 1999 28.5-foot Terry fifth wheel trailer!
(key this into the command line of your browser to view the image
on-line! www.keithlistoe.ca/traileroutside_slideout_side.jpg)

That was about six hundred people for the Siloam Mission and about two hundred supported by Lutheran Urban Ministry in December of 2008. I concluded that it was approximately $10 per plate for a catered meal.

This was the greatest material change in my life. I am now a content eight year old with forty-three years' experience; a half physically dead miracle man walking. Oh, God is great! I can unequivocally write that the material change everyone thinks would be the greatest for them is to win a lottery of millions of dollars. The only change this would make in your life is an exponential increase in worries, anxiety, stress and fear, which is the furthest possible way to a life of contentment. To be content, you must remove all reasons for worries, anxiety, stress and fear from your life. If you have sufficient money and material personal possessions to survive, you should be content! On the other hand, you will be in a position to begin making your life one of complete joy and happiness!

The best thing to remember for this change is that you do not need to wait for anything to happen to you; you can easily make the choice now to remove the money and material personal possessions above what you require to survive. To make the choice for a change is completely more positive than having to accept and handle any changes that occur to you. I said I was writing this in complete truthfulness and honesty. I have one change that I really struggle with, which is to just accept and continue on without becoming angry, upset or depressed, because of the injuries I incurred from the SUV striking me on December 10, 2005.

After I misused and abused the miraculous healing and recovery Jesus worked for me from the four massive hemorrhagic strokes in December of 2002. This misuse and abuse could only have been for my own glory, not the glory to God. I am now unable to skate and play goal. I wanted to play goal well into being a senior citizen. However, I am alive and still able to do miraculous things physically, so I have nothing to complain or feel bad about. Thank you, God! Yes, in conclusion, regardless of the change, be thankful. Once you discover the power of thanksgiving, you will be able to get through everything in life! The following are the times I ran up four floors, and now eight floors, at Manitoba Hydro Place, 360 Portage Avenue in Winnipeg, Mb.

Date	Time in seconds 1st@ 7 AM	Time in seconds 2nd @ 10 AM	Time in seconds 3rd@ 2 PM			
Tues., April 30, 2013	44.00	45.90	44.50	11.0	9.0	
Date	**Time in seconds 1st@ 7 AM**	**Time in seconds 2nd @ 8:30 AM**	**Time in seconds 3rd@ 10 AM**	**Time in seconds 4th@ 11:30 AM**	**Time in seconds 5th@ 1 PM**	**Time in seconds 6th@ 2:30 PM**

Thurs., July 25, 2013	37.02	36.74	37.93	37.16	35.98	34.68
Wed., August 14, 2013	35.82	35.27	34.64	34.00	42.30	34.36
	Time in seconds 1st@ 7 AM	**Time in seconds 2nd@ 11 AM**	**Time in seconds 3rd@ 3 PM**			
Wed., September 25, 2013	87.47 1st timing of running 8 floors!	88.16	87.85			
Wed., October 23, 2013	82.87	80.12	79.77 first broke 80 seconds running 8 floors continu-ously!			

Tues., November 05, 2013	80.78 delayed stopping time because I missed the button on the first attempt!	70.76 most miracu-lous time after returning from Dr. appoint-ment	77.30			
Wed., March 26, 2014	78.96	75.69	74.48			
Wed., April 23, 2014	80.09	78.62	75.95			
Mon., September 08, 2014	74.89	76.24	77.31			

Wed., September 17, 2014	79.14	78.96	79.09 I started running as a woman running stepped onto the eighth floor. I ran faster than her up to the seven- teenth floor!			
Thurs., September 18, 2014	77.59	78.67	78.46			
Fri., September 19, 2014	77.37	77.57	81.31			
Mon., September 22, 2014	76.22	78.69	78.27			
Mon., September 22, 2014	76.22	76.22	76.22			

Tues., September 23, 2014	80.99	80.16	79.10		
Wed., September 24, 2014	78.73	78.39	78.79		
Thurs., September 25, 2014	79.82	79.40	79.00		
Fri., September 26, 2014	77.97	78.74	76.95		
Tues., September 30, 2014	81.41	80.08	80.75		
Wed., October 1, 2014	79.11	78.80	77.99		
Mon., October 6, 2014	78.98	79.38	77.22		
Tues., October 7, 2014	78.78	78.09	79.69		

Wed., October 8, 2014	80.89	79.21	78.06			
Thurs., October 9, 2014	79.63	78.96	78.22			
Fri., October 10, 2014	81.03	75.91	33.07 (12th) 67.55 (17th)			

For the first two years after being released from the hospital on April 7, 2003, I could count the number of times I felt hungry on two hands and had concluded that I would only feel hungry if I ate too much for a meal. I decided that it was logical and reasonable to continue eating three meals per day at breakfast, lunch and supper; but I was putting on weight after the first year, so I decided to try not eating one meal per day. I stopped eating lunch with no change in my feelings of hunger, but my weight became constant at approximately 150 pounds. Thank God, my children accepted my suggestion for a present of a power food slicer, so I would not have to slice cheese or fresh vegetables one-handed to make lasagna, my favorite recipe.

I started to cook suppers to once a month after buying fifty single serving freezer containers. I cook using a large Dutch oven full of KLM-n-CD (Keith Listoe Macaroni and Cheese Deluxe) or KLS-n-MSD (Keith Listoe Spaghetti and Meat Sauce Deluxe). This changed, however, in 2012, when I took my tricycle to Spiritwood, Sk. I thought I would be able to ride my tricycle out to my favorite lake, which is Little Shell Lake east of Spiritwood off highway #3. I made my first attempt riding to Mildred after successfully riding my tricycle out to the house of my best friend, Raymond Dumas, in one hour on a gravel road. My legs were completely exhausted before getting anywhere close to

Mildred, because it was uphill all the way riding my tricycle for fifty minutes. It only took fifteen minutes to ride back to Spiritwood! I was greatly disappointed that it was impossible for me to ride my tricycle out to Little Shell Lake.

I decided to spend all of my time working on the content for www.ondemandwisdom.com. I made the mistake of continuing to eat too much trail mix daily without any physical exercise, and I only had sweat pants to wear, which did not provide me the indication that I was putting on weight. I had taken my 32-inch waist shorts to wear riding my tricycle. When I returned to Winnipeg in September 2012, I could not put on a pair of my 34-inch pants. I had to buy some new pants that were 40 inches to get them done up with all the weight I had put on. I decided to donate all of my clothing to the Lutheran Urban Ministry to sell in their Christmas store.

I decided to go on a three week fast in February 2013 to see if that would enable me to lose the weight and inches I had put on. I lost the majority of the weight and the majority of the inches, but I found some old 34-inch blue jeans I missed donating to LUM. I could do up the button, but I could not do up the zipper. I had to purchase a new suit, shirts and ties to wear to Tyler's iron ring ceremony on March 19, 2013, and to Brandi's wedding on July 6, 2013. The pants were a 36-inch waist, but they still had to let out the butt somewhat to fit properly.

I was in peak physical condition in 2002 when I miraculously survived the four massive hemorrhagic strokes. I was thirty-nine years old and still played hockey in any position except goaltending. The only player on my team that could out skate me was only eighteen years old! The first question a doctor asked me in the hospital was, "What kind of a house do you live in?" I answered, "A two-story house." She asked, "With a full flight of stairs?" I answered, "Yes, it is a two-story house." She said, "You better plan on selling that house and buying a wheelchair accessible bungalow, because you will never climb stairs again if you are even able to walk."

After weeks of physiotherapy on my left leg and sitting in a wheelchair, I asked if I could try standing up. The therapist was very firm that it was too soon for me to try that. That night I noticed there was a solid railing around my bed with enough open space that I could try walking by holding it. I successfully did this, getting the idea that I will really shock my physiotherapist tomorrow by telling her not to get excited and grab me as I stand up out of my wheelchair and walk past her! She was so shocked I successfully did this that I thought I might have to pick her up off the floor!

I received my first day pass out of the hospital on February 14, 2003. The first thing I did when I arrived home was go up the stairs to my bedroom. I had to ask Teri to help me go down, because there was no handrail on the right side of the stairway going down. Mark and Dad put a railing up on this stairway and the stairway in the garage. After I started working for Manitoba Hydro, my cubicle was on the fourth floor at 820 Taylor Avenue. The cafeteria was in the basement and one day I had the idea to try taking the stairs up to the fourth floor after the morning coffee break, as my way to get some exercise instead of playing hockey. I knew I could not skate anymore. I was completely out of breath by the time I made it up to the fourth floor and it took a very long time; but it felt great to exercise like this with my disabilities! I wanted to reduce the amount of time it took me to go up the stairs though, so at noon, I decided to try taking two steps at a time. I was just as out of breath, but the time was greatly reduced and I felt more comfortable taking two steps at a time than one. I was hooked on this as my new way to exercise to keep myself in peak physical condition. I began going up the stairs like this three times a day after each coffee break and lunch hour.

I received a wristwatch with a stopwatch built in for Christmas, 2004. I was often arriving on the fourth floor before my co-workers got out of the elevator. I had the idea to time myself going up the stairs and then up in the elevator to see if I could possibly beat it up to the fourth floor without it stopping at another floor to let someone out. I learned that if I started timing the elevator once the doors were closed, it took twenty-six seconds to reach the fourth floor. The fastest I timed myself going up the stairs was twenty-eight seconds, but there was one day that I watched a co-worker, Ryan Armstrong, enter the elevator and started going up the stairs as the door began to close. I was totally shocked when I was on the fourth floor before Ryan arrived in the elevator. I asked him, "What floor did someone get out on?" He answered, "None; I was alone in the elevator!" Quite miraculous for being told to sell my two-story house because I would never climb stairs again.

I really wanted to know if I would be able to run again. In the spring of 2005, I was out in the park kicking a soccer ball back and forth with my son, Tyler, and he accidentally kicked the ball off to my left side. With a reflex reaction, I ran over to stop it before it went past me. I was totally shocked and thankful that I was able to run. I instructed Tyler to continue kicking the ball off to my side to force me to have to run to stop it before it got past me. I asked my son, Cody, to come with me to the 100-meter racetrack in the schoolyard one day in the summer of 2005, to time me running the 100-meter dash. He walked down to the finish line as I lined up at the starting line. He hollered ready, set, go, and I took off running. I almost tripped just after starting because my left toe hooked on my right heal. Somehow, I managed to keep my balance and completed the 100-meter dash in twenty-one seconds. Another miraculous accomplishment for a half physically dead 42-year-old miracle man running!

I was out of shape for the first time in my life and I knew I was not able to run anymore; but I started my stairs exercise, from the eighth floor up to the twelfth floor, three times daily again on April 30, 2013, at 360 Portage Avenue, where I now work. However, I do not have the same drive to compete with the elevator to improve my time so dramatically like I did in 2004-2005. Jesus Christ has convinced me that he wants to reveal his power, might, abilities, love and existence through me, by making me so successful doing physical activities now being a half physically dead miracle man running. I set the goal that I would have Cody time me running the 100-meter dash again if I broke thirty-six seconds running up four floors of stairs. I broke thirty-six seconds on Friday, July 26, 2013. Cody surprised me by videotaping the run on Saturday July 27, 2013, completing the 100-meter dash again in 34.04 seconds. Here is the video: www.keithlistoe.ca/IMG_0612.MOV . His comment of, "Why is your right hand going around like a windmill?" I answered, "I have no idea it is, because I am concentrating 100 percent on moving my left leg to run. You can understand now why I am completely more comfortable running up the stairs, where I have the handrail to hold onto."

This provided me the idea for what I have named the stroke-fit system. This is a 100-meter racetrack with a handrail beside it that has a roller-bearing mounted hand grip on top of it. In addition, it has an automatic timer that will start as you pass the first support post of the handrail, and stop as you pass the final support post of the handrail. A large digital display of the time would hang down at the end of the track. In the summer of 2008, a fellow stroke survivor stopped attending the monthly meetings for The Next Step peer support group I had facilitated. I learned it was because he had been evicted from his apartment, so he had nowhere to live. I further learned he had moved into the Siloam Mission facility and I went there to talk to him. I really wondered what my life would be like if I was not able to work like I did before I miraculously survived four massive hemorrhagic strokes in December, 2002. I made an appointment with an agent at Welfare Canada to inquire how much I would receive if I had to go on to welfare. I was told I would receive $340 per month. I quickly asked, "How much would I receive for accommodations?" because my current rent was $700-800 per month. The answer was nothing, you would only receive $340 per month! I did not need to do any math and I knew I would be living out on the street, starving, if I had to live on welfare in Winnipeg, Mb.

As a personal challenge, I decided to determine if I could live on only $340 per month after paying my rent, so I put myself on this monthly budget in August 2008. It did not take long for me to realize, I could not afford the $10-plus per week to continue bowling. I had my monthly spending under control by December to return to it, so I bowled for my team until the end of the season. That way, they could try to find a new teammate to bowl with them the next year. I decided to stop bowling for other reasons than financial. The late nights did not suit the other changes in my life to enable me to have my Daily Devotional readings each morning before I caught the bus to work at 6:15 a.m. My shower, breakfast and Daily Devotional readings take approximately three hours, so I had to wake up at 3:15 a.m. To get my now required eight hours of sleep, I had to be in bed by 7 p.m.

Jesus Christ selects the scripture passage he wants me to read as his message to me each day. By using the Web App I hired someone to develop for me, you can see them here: www.ondemandwisdom.com/Daily_Devotional_Readings.htm. This has been the perfect learning in my life to now be living content: That we humans seek, desire and are required to be living now at the end of the age! I decided to change my work hours to 7 a.m. to 3:30 p.m., which enabled me to catch the number 63 bus to and from work at times with very few passengers. This was initiated after my Handi Transit ride home from work in January 2009 never showed up after I had phoned them three times and being told it would be there in ten minutes each time.

In December 2010, I finally changed all of my personally recorded ringtones for my KRZR1 Motorola cell phone for each of my 210 contacts to reduce the bit rate quality to make smaller files, so all 210 of them would fit on my cell phone to be used as the ringtone for each of my contacts. Each ringtone was a contact's name, so I had hands free audio caller ID to suit my disability of only having one hand to use to do anything, making it impossible to pick up my phone to look at it if I was holding something else when my phone rang. In addition, I bought a wireless Bluetooth headset to use with this cell phone, which only required the push of the button on my left ear to answer the phone or to make a phone call using voice dialing. There is one situation I have found myself in that it was impossible for me to answer my phone, which is if I am standing up on the bus, having to hold onto the handrail to avoid falling over. If I am wearing the Bluetooth headset, I can let go long enough to push the button to answer the phone and grab hold of the handrail again before falling over.

After I made the decision that I wanted the most overwhelming and intense feelings of puppy love for Jesus Christ to mature into being in a giving from my heart, true love, faith relationship with Jesus Christ. I had the ideas to change my meal time grace to the following to better emphasize my desire to do all I am able to promote and grow the body of Jesus Christ worldwide.

Come Lord Jesus, be my guest. Thank you for this great tasting and abundant food. Please bless my body, heart, soul, mind and strength my complete being, to your body's use, through the book The Perfect Life. Please bless this food, to my body's use!

Amen.

MANAGING EXPECTATIONS

I am convinced that if I did not manage my expectations now, I would too easily become depressed or suicidal. The psychiatrist that locked me up in 2011 refuses to see me now as his patient. That is, unless I go to see him through the emergency room again, as I saw him the first time. I'm sure it was because I told him that the positive I had found from unsuccessfully trying to castrate myself was having him become my psychiatrist and to have one to tell the absolute truth. I now know of the perfect life of complete joy and happiness we humans seek, desire and are required to be living now, at the end of the age. I now live the perfect life of complete joy and happiness, free of worry, anxiety, stress and fear! He could not argue with me because he has never seen anyone so joyful and happy before in his life. His offer to prescribe me a medication that I refused could not make anyone as joyful and happy as I am.

The first psychiatrist, my family doctor, had seen me after I asked her to castrate me after I was unsuccessful on my initial attempt in April of 2006. I became depressed taking an anti-depressant that I expected erectile dysfunction as a side effect from it. Because I now know how I could be successful, having only gross manual dexterity in my left hand that would require gross actions, I will not be making any future attempts to castrate myself or attain erectile dysfunction. However, I fear the greatest disappointment for me living half physically dead will soon be upon me. That is my oldest daughter, Brandi, will begin a family. I know from experience with my grandnephew, Rylin Listoe, in 2010, I am not able to pick up and hold a baby, or even really enjoy playing with a baby, because I must bend over to play with the baby lying on the floor, which is the most difficult and exhausting thing for me to do. In addition, I know that I am able to fly anywhere around the world by myself without getting lost by requesting a wheelchair, but it is impossible for me to go out to Winkler, Mb, by myself where Brandi now lives, because there is no public transportation between Winnipeg and there.

After having the fifth surgery on my head on Tuesday, October 13, 2009, to put in a titanium plate to cover the dent in my head from the section of my skull removed in the third emergency operation in December 2002, I began to use the phrase, '*I have a steel trap of a memory now*', which I use both figuratively and literally. I have the extreme positive change of remembering numbers now, but I'm extremely absentminded in remembering most everything else. I learned how to create reminders in Microsoft Outlook, with recorded audio files for what the reminder is for, so I do not have to read the screen to know what I need to do. I can hear it wherever I am or whatever I am doing at my desk, or in my apartment. I have made the change in my life to use this to create a reminder for everything I need to do to ensure I do not forget doing anything now with my absentmindedness. My greatest challenge now is to remember to create a reminder for everything, but over the years of doing this, it is becoming a habit; so I'm less likely to forget now. If I dial a phone number, it is there in my memory. If I used my credit card over the phone, it is in my memory now. I don't need to look at my credit card again to know the number. I also use alarms on my iPhone to be able to hear the alarm go off to remind me to look at my iPhone to see what the alarm is for, and for what I need to do. Creating recurring reminders in Outlook for birthdays has been the best way to surprise so many people in my life now that I remembered theirs or their child's birthday!

I have come up with the following idea for my own personal therapy to improve my memory, concentration and physical vision: I must see the following list of landmarks or businesses on my bus rides to or home from work each day. To work, 155 places:

1.   Hospital

2.   Thrift Store

3.   Shoppers Drug Mart

4.   Giant Tiger

5.   Auto Parts

6.   WM trash bin now Progressive trash bin

7.   Safeway

8.   light standard

9.   McDonald's

10.   Petro Canada

11.   Applebee's

12.   Earl's

13.   Monty's now moco

14.   Running Room

15.   KFC

16.   RBC ATM

17.   Thatcher north

18.   Capri Motel

19.   A&W

20.   Fabricland

21.   Fort Garry

22.   Chancellor

23.   Pembina village shopping centre

24.   Chancellor Square yellow sign

25.   Pembina @ University crescent

26.   Petland

27.   Dollarama

28.   Singleton's

29.   blank white sign Office Depot

30.   Pembina @ Plaza

31.   Napa Auto

32.   Value Village

33.   Crescent

34.   Pembina on the Red

35.   Alter Ego

36.   Visions

37.   Arizona Plaza

38.   Tony Roma's

39.   Tim Horton's

40.   Winnipeg Technical College

41.   Alter Ego

42.   Ken Pass Law

43.   Landmark Gallery

44.   Piston Ring

45.   Cottage Bakery

46.   Holiday Inn

47.   Archdiocese of Winnipeg

48.   Connections blank sign now

49.   Pembina @ Fletcher

50.   T.H. Dang Restaurant

51.   OSI

52.   Kelsey Apartments

53.   blue roof strip mall

54.   Chicken Delight

55.   Safeway

56.   brown roof strip mall

57.   Hakim Optical

58.   Rexall

59.   Pembina @ Oakenwald

60.   RBC

61.   Pembina @ Point Road

62.   Perth's now Dulux Paints

63.   Petro Canada now Cloutiers Auto Service

64.   CG Power systems Canada Inc.

65.   Royal Realty

66.   Job Works

67.   Shoppers Drug Mart

68.   KFC now 7 Eleven

69.   Pancake House

70.   Pembi Football

71.   Fountain Tire

72.   Manitoba Hydro on Taylor

73.   southwest transitway @ Jubilee

74.   Price Choppers

75.   Reflections

76.   Round Table if tracks clear

77.   Castrol if tracks clear

78.   Kessay if tracks clear

79.   Just Imagine if tracks clear

80.   Cambrian Credit Union if tracks clear

81.   Fort Rouge Station

82.   Lohas Restaurant if tracks clear

83.   Carpet Barn if tracks clear

84.   McMunn & Yates if tracks clear

85.   Quality inn & Suites

86.   McDonald's on Pembina

87.   Tim Horton's on Pembina

88.   Golden Boy

89.   McDonald's on Osborne

90.   Deaf Center Manitoba

91.   Osborne Station

92.   Burger King

93.   River and Osborne steeple

94.   Village Laundry

95.   Antiques

96.   Sukho Thai

97.   Osborne Village Motor Inn

98.   Dollarama

99.   Gord's bike

100.   #6 Donald

101.   Winnipeg Racquet Club

102.   Journey's End

103.   Design Manitoba

104.   Harkness Station

105.   Winnipeg Winter Club

106.   Gracie Humaita

107.   Museum of Human Rights

108.   train overpass

109.   Mayfair @Queen Elizabeth

110.   Church steeple

111.   east side of midtown bridge monument

112.   Main @ Assiniboine

113.   VJ's DRIVE INN

114.   Main @ Broadway Union Station

115.   Union Station

116.   Fountain Tire on York

117.   Earl's

118.   High & Lonesome Club

119.   the sign source on St Mary

120.   Hargrave & St Mary steeple

121.   CDI College

122.   Graham @ Garry Winnipeg Square

123.   Manitoba Hydro Place

124.   Tim Horton's on Graham

125.   Winnipeg Square

126.   Holy Trinity Hall steeple

127.   RBC Fort and Portage

128.   Portage @ Donald MTS center

129.   Dollarama

130.   Carlton skywalk

131.   Donald skywalk

132.   Best Western

133.   Calvary Temple

134.   Vaughan skywalk

135.   Tim Horton's in Portage Place Mall

136.   RBC

137.   Portage @ Edmonton Portage Place

138.   Hakim Optical on Portage

139.   Tim Horton's on Portage at Vaughan

140.   Holiday Inn & Suites

141.   Colony

142.   Booth University College

143.   University of Winnipeg Steeple

144.   Balmoral Station

145.   #47 bus departs Balmoral station at 6:34A.M.

146.   #160 bus departs Balmoral station at 6:36A.M.

147.   Ellice

148.   NRC CNRC

149.   TLC

150.   Ellice @ Edmonton

151.   MEDICAL CENTRE

152.   Carlton @ Portage north

153.   Carlton Inn

154.   Portage south

155.   City Place parking sign

This is a greatly reduced and changed listing after the rapid transit system became operational. Some places are much more difficult, if not impossible, to see in the spring or summer because of the leaves on the trees. In addition, some places are only visible if there are no train cars on the Fort Rouge tracks, but I allow myself to count seeing them if I remember to try seeing them when the tracks are covered with train cars. There are also days riding the bus that I am unable to see the majority of these places, because the bus is overloaded with people. When the bus is overcrowded, these folks block the front window from my regular seat on the right front seat and my view out the left side windows. In addition, there are some buses that have the windows covered with some kind of decals, which makes it very difficult to see clearly enough to count my locations. On the way home from work there are 140 places:

1.   Carlton skywalk

2.   Calvary Temple steeple

3.   Tim Horton's in Portage Place mall

4.   Vaughan skywalk

5.   RBC

6   Hargrave @ St Mary steeple

7   City Place parking sign

8   Carlton Inn

9   RBC Convention Center

10   Hull's books

11   Graham @ Hargrave

12   Holy Trinity Hall steeple

13   Donald skywalk

14   Best Western

15   Smith MTS center

16   RBC Fort and Portage

17   Fort Winnipeg Square

18   Winnipeg Square canopy

19   Tim Horton's on Graham

20   CDI College

21   Main @ St Mary

22   Union Station

23   High & Lonesome club

24   the Museum of Human Rights

25   the sign source on St Mary

26   Earl's

27   Fountain Tire on York

28   Main @ Broadway Union Station

29   VJ's Drive Inn

30   Assiniboine

31   train overpass

32	east side of midtown bridge monument
33	Queen Elizabeth @ Stradbrook
34	Church steeple
35	Gracie Humaita
36	Winnipeg Winter Club
37	Golden Boy landmark
38	Harkness Station
39	Dollarama
40	Gord's Cycle
41	Journey's end
42	Manitoba Design
43	Winnipeg Racquet Club
44	#6 Donald
45	River @ Osborne steeple
46	Burger King
47	Osborne Station
48	McDonalds on Osborne

49   Village Laundry

50   Antiques

51   Sukho Thai Restaurant

52   Osborne Village Motor Inn

53   Deaf Center Manitoba on Pembina

54   Tim Horton's on Pembina

55   McDonalds on Pembina

56   Fort Rouge Station

57   Lohas Restaurant if tracks clear

58   Carpet Barn if tracks clear

59   McMunn & Yates if tracks clear

60   Quality Inn & Suites

61   Jubilee

62   Castrol if tracks clear

63   Kessay if tracks clear

64   Just Imagine if tracks clear

65   Cambrian Credit Union if tracks clear

66   Round Table if tracks clear

67   Fountain Tire

68   Manitoba Hydro on Taylor

69   Price Choppers

70   Reflections

71   pancake House

72   Pembi football

73   Pembina @ Windermere

74   KFC now 7 Eleven

75   Perth's now Dulux Paints

76   Safeway

77   Shoppers Drug Mart

78   CG Power Systems Canada Inc.

79   Job Works

80   Royal Realty

81   Petro Canada now Cloutiers Auto Service

82   McGillivray

83	RBC
84	Holiday Inn
85	Rexall
86	Hakim Optical
87	Chicken Delight
88	Cottage Bakery
89	brown roof strip mall
90	Piston Ring
91	blue roof strip mall
92	Kelsey Apartments
93	OSI
94	T.H Dang Restaurant
95	Clarence
96	connections blank sign now
97	Archdiocese of Winnipeg
98	Landmark Gallery
99	Chevrier

100	Tim Horton's
101	Tony Roma's
102	Ken Pass Law
103	Winnipeg Technical College
104	Alter Ego Sports
105	Napa Auto parts
106	Value Village
107	A&W
108	Fort Garry
109	Alter Ego
110	Arizona Plaza
111	Visions
112	Pembina on the Red
113	Capri Motel
114	blank white sign Office Depot
115	Fabricland
116	Earls

117   McDonalds

118   Petland

119   Dollarama

120   Pembina @ Plaza

121   Singleton's

122   Petro Canada

123   Pembina @ University crescent

124   Pembina Village Shopping Centre

125   Chancellor

126   Chancellor Square yellow sign

127   KFC

128   RBC ATM

129   Running Room

130   Applebee's

131   Safeway

132   Thatcher

133   Thrift Store

134	Auto Parts
135	Hospital
136	Monty's now moco
137	light standard
138	Shoppers Drug Mart
139	Giant Tiger
140	WM trash bin now Progressive trash bin

I also must remember to see each of the listed places and bus stops on my bus ride to church each Sunday morning. There are 57 places in total:

1.   Hospital

2.   Thrift Store

3.   Shoppers Drug Mart

4.   Giant Tiger

5.   Auto Parts

6.   WM trash bin now Progressive trash bin

7.   Safeway

8.   Light standard

9.   McDonalds

10.   Petro Canada

11.   Applebee's

12.   Earls

13.   Monty's now moco

14.   Running room

15.   KFC

16.   RBC ATM

17.   Southpark park & ride

18.   Southpark south

19.   Markham

20.   Pembina @ Dartmouth Victoria Hospital

21.   Dartmouth south

22.   Tim Horton's

23.   DQ

24.   Church Steeple

25.   Bison north

26.   Bison

27.   Fairfield

28.   Bairdmore north

29.   Boston Pizza

30.   Bairdmore

31.   Fountain Tire

32.   Shoppers Drug Mart

33.   Saigon John's

34.   Greencrest

35.   Burger King

36.   McDonald's

37.   Richmond West sign

38.   Safeway now knocked down!

39.   Singleton's

40.   Killarney @ Pembina east

41.   Baylor @ Killarney

42.   Mount Allison

43.   Bryn Mawr

44.   Leeds

45.   Dalhousie

46.   Petro Canada

47.   Dalhousie @ Bromley

48.   Ryerson elementary school

49.   Ryerson

50.   Rochester

51.   St. Edmund's

52.   Milikin

53.   St. Dunstan's

54.   Rutgers

55.   Dalhousie @ Perdue

56.   Silverstone

57.   Epiphany Lutheran Church

In addition, the following list of places, 84 in all, is from work to the St. Vital Mall:

1.   Carlton skywalk

2.   Calvary Temple steeple

3.   Tim Horton's in Portage Place mall

4.   Vaughan skywalk

5.   RBC

6.   RBC Convention center

7.   City Place parking sign

8.   Donald skywalk

9.   Best Western

10.   Dollarrama

11.   Fort

12.   RBC Fort @ Portage

13.   Main at Pioneer

14.   Winnipeg Square

15.   Main at St Mary

16.   Union Station

17.   CDI College

18.   Holy Trinity Hall steeple

19.   High & Lonesome club

20.   the sign source on St Mary

21.   Hargrave @ St Mary steeple

22.   Museum of Human Rights

23.   Earl's

24.   Fountain Tire on York

25.   VJ's drive in

26.   train overpass

27.   east side of midtown bridge monument

28.   Queen Elizabeth at Stradbrook

29.   church steeple

30.   Golden boy

31.   St Mary at Marion

32.   Walmer

33.   Enfield

34.   Nelson McIntyre collegiate

35.   Highfield

36.   Red Roof restaurant

37.   Coniston

38.   JB transmission

39.   Carrier

40.   Visual Productions

41.   Fifth

42.   Morier

43.   Midland Appliance

44.   Vivian

45.   Perth's

46.   Prosperity monument

47.   church steeple

48.   St. Anne's at Blenheim

49.   Lorraine

50.   Victory

51.   McDonald's on St Anne's

52. Sherwood

53. DQ on St Anne's

54. RBC

55. Hilvadore apartments

56. Regal

57. Superstore

58. Fermor

59. Safeway

60. St. Anne's at Niakwa

61. Chicken Delight

62. Morrow

63. Ashton

64. Barton

65. Portland

66. Berrydale

67. Sadler

68. Hindley

69.   Worthington

70.   Beliveau

71.   Beliveau at St. Anne's

72.   Behnke

73.   Beachtree

74.   Kearney

75.   Eric

76.   Dakota

77.   A&W

78.   Dollarrama

79.   Dakota Collegiate

80.   Dakota at Chesterfield

81.   Bishop Grandin

82.   Tim Horton's

83.   Shopper's Drug Mart

84.   Bishop Grandin south

And home from the St. Vital mall 44 places:

1.   Tim Horton's

2.   Shopper's Drug Mart

3.   Beliveau

4.   Dakota at St. Marie's

5.   Dakota Collegiate

6.   St. Marie's at Arden

7.   Chesterfield

8.   A&W

9.   KFC

10.   Dollarama

11.   London Drugs

12.   Bishop Grandin at Glen Meadows

13.   River

14.   Bishop Grandin at Pembina crossing

15.   Dollarama

16.   Petland

17.   singletons

18.   Fabricland

19.   A&W

20.   Fort Garry

21.   Capri Motel

22.   blank white sign Office Depot

23.   Pembina

24.   Earls

25.   McDonald's

26.   Petro Canada

27.   Pembina at University crescent

28.   Pembina at Chancellor

29.   Pembina village shopping Centre

30.   Chancellor square yellow sign

31.   KFC

32.   RBC ATM

33.   Running room

34.   Applebee's

35.	Safeway
36.	Thatcher
37.	Thrift Store
38.	Auto Parts
39.	Hospital
40.	Monty's now moco
41.	Light standard
42.	Shoppers Drug Mart
43.	Giant Tiger
44.	WM trash bin now Progressive trash bin

ANGER

Do not allow yourself to become angry because of a change that occurs. If you let yourself become angry, you have eliminated the possibility that you will have any opportunity to find a positive in the change; and you eliminate the possibility that you could make future positive changes to make the change positive! Anger locks you into negativity.

EXPECTED FUTURE CHANGES

To suit my disabilities now, I live in an apartment to avoid having to shovel any snow in the winter to clear my sidewalk or driveway. I truly miss the work I can do in the yard though, so I have had an idea for how I could build a house that would not require me to shovel any snow. It is also temperature controlled like the Manitoba Hydro Place building. That's the most comfortable place I have ever been in with my dislike of forced air heating and cooling systems. These systems cause drafts that chill my half physically dead body too much for me to stand. I originally had the idea how I could construct a good portion of this house myself only having the full use of my right-hand, but I have let my common sense prevail. I will not try to construct any parts of this house myself, but only work directly with a new-found friend, Alcide Bouchard, who is a house designer, to be sure my ideas for this house are correct. I am positive I could build a wall of a house if I bought a power miter saw and air nailer. But this is only possible if I save enough money over the next ten years. If I am able to build my own house, I will not include a ninety-two step straight stairway. That way, I would not have to turn corners running my stair climbing exercise such as at Manitoba Hydro Place, 360 Portage Avenue, but will include a waist-high handrail in the basement walls to hold onto while running laps around the basement.

I completed moving into a main floor apartment on June 30, 2013- July 1, 2013. I learned the shower head is located in the right, correct side of the tub as I step into it, because this makes it possible for me to hold my left hand up above my head by grabbing the shower curtain bar and spraying the water into my left under arm without problems. I will not be building my own house to suit my disabilities or just to have a back yard for a garden. I will remain living in this main floor apartment with sufficient room to store my tricycle in the living room out of the way of the patio doors. I have a dining room table, and a hide-a-bed. My computer desk is now in my bedroom. However, if I do receive sufficient income from this book, I will buy a condo in Israel and become the peacemaker I was created to be, which is my true purpose in life here on Earth! In addition, this will enable me to have $1,105,405.41 to hire IDERS to develop the charity survival RFID system.

As written in Chapter Six, *Positively a Near Perfect World,* I will also be able to give $1,105,405.41 to a total list of thirty-seven entities including myself as two, but this includes using such funds to build a new office building for the Stroke Recovery Association of Manitoba SAM, which would include my idea for a stroke fit system. This system has a 100- meter racetrack with a handrail, which has a roller-bearing mounted hand grip on top of it. It also has an automatic timer, which would start as the person passes the first upright support of the handrail. It would automatically stop when the person passes the last upright support of the handrail. There would be a large digital display of the time at the end of the handrail. If I do not receive like this, I know from experience spending just over $12,000 in a month on three different Facebook advertisements for:

www.ondemandwisdom.com/Daily_Devotional_Readings.htm,
www.ondemandwisdom.com and
www.ondemandwisdom.com/The_NKJV_Bible.html,

achieving a total combined reach of 39,000,000 or more that I can afford to pay the Facebook advertising to just give *The Human Mind Positively Can: The Power of the Subconscious!* away and have no expectations of doing or giving any of these written ideas. Otherwise, if I do not meet these expectations, I will surely become depressed and or suicidal. I did have confirmation of my idea that I could get a full night's sleep free of feeling unbearably frozen on the left side of my body by having a trial sleep in the quiet room on the eighteenth floor of Manitoba Hydro Place on December 16, 2013!

The bed in the quiet room on the 18th floor of Manitoba Hydro Place!
(key this into the command line of your browser to view the
image on-line! www.keithlistoe.ca/IMG_0043.JPG)

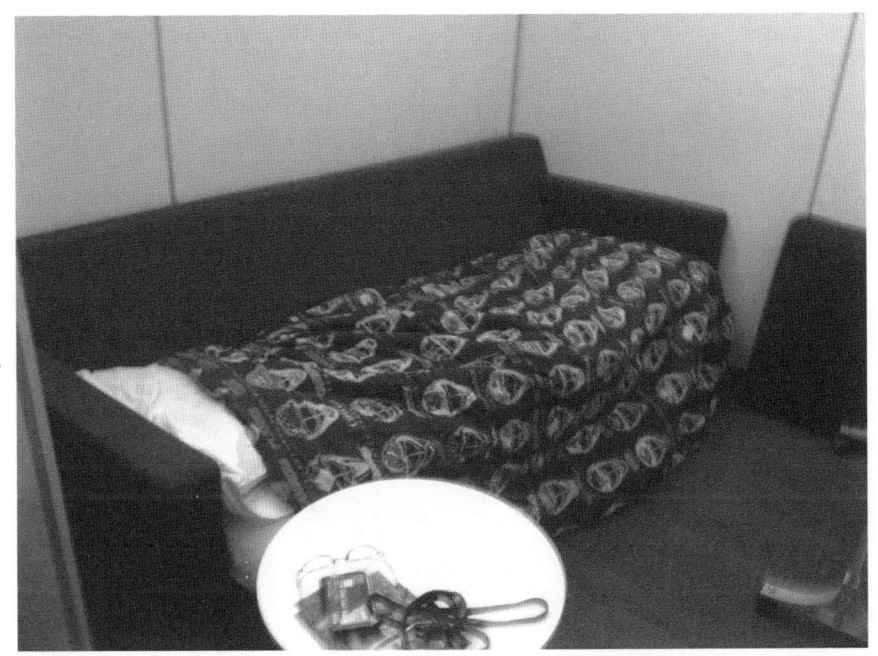

My made bed at Manitoba Hydro Place!
(key this into the command line of your browser to view the
image on-line! www.keithlistoe.ca/IMG_0044.JPG)

Cody's heater at the foot of my bed in my apartment!
(key this into the command line of your browser to view the
image on-line! www.keithlistoe.ca/IMG_0035.JPG)

My desire to build my own house based on the geothermal heating and
cooling system used at Manitoba Hydro Place is greater than ever now. When
I do, I will no longer need the heater at the foot of my bed to prevent feeling
unbearably frozen while sleeping in the apartment I am now living in. I have

made further changes to my bed in the apartment to not require the heater at the foot of my bed to avoid feeling unbearably frozen, by placing an electric blanket under the mattress. In addition, I could sit in my new house for hours working on my computer without feeling unbearably frozen on the left side of my body. I tried using an electric blanket in my apartment, but it is much less than satisfactory. My house plan has a double concrete foundation with a TBD width space between them to be used as an air-to-air heat exchange of the fresh air drawn into the house from the south side solar-heated space. This will include a solar chimney surrounding a wood-burning fireplace chimney. There would be a concrete floor on top of the interior concrete foundation walls. All of these concrete walls and the floor would have geothermal heating pipes running through them. There would be a raised floor over the main concrete floor under which the fresh air would be drawn through to the solar chimney. The front entrance would be on the north side of the house. The front door would be a set of thick, insulated double French oak doors with a narrow window on either side.

As you enter the foyer, there will be a coat closet on the right side and a sitting bench on the left side over a shoe rack. There will also be a second set of double French doors of oak, glass and brass. The cathedral ceiling will have clerestory windows in the peak. The sun would shine through these, and through a stained glass window of an outdoor scene. This picture window will be above the doors to the ceiling. This would enable the inside of the front doors to be heated by the sun in the wintertime by painting the inside of the doors flat black. The floor of the front foyer would be slate tiles, which would also absorb the sun's heat in the wintertime. I have not thought in complete detail enough yet how to complete this house design, but it would have a stairway up to the clerestory windows. There would also be an elevator to go back down to the main floor and into the basement. The fireplace would be on the right side of this stairway. There is a second floor behind this stairway and above the kitchen only to separate the main floor from the glass wall above this floor to heat the solar chimney. There will be a waterfall humidifier/dehumidifier on the left side of the fireplace. The fireplace would be finished with dry pack stone work. The waterfall would fall into the bathroom.

Here is the electric blanket under my chair platform!
(key this into the command line of your browser to view the
image on-line! www.keithlistoe.ca/IMG_0045.jpg)

The exterior main floor walls are based on the R2000 design concept of a 2X6 insulated wall, unbroken vapor barrier, a 2-inch space then a 2X4-inch insulated wall with broken vapor barrier by the electrical outlets with receptacles and switches. The sidewalk and driveway would be heated to avoid having to shovel any snow now that I'm one-handed. I know that the main floor apartment feels cold because there is no heated apartment below it to warm the floor. The electric baseboard heaters are not able to warm the entire floor. I have made a number of changes to live in this main floor apartment without feeling unbearably frozen either while sitting still for hours working on my computer or while sleeping. I put the electric blanket under my chair platform with the blanket folded up over the front of the platform, so my feet are directly on top of the electric blanket. In addition, I wear my winter boots and a new pair of insulated ski pants.

I replaced the old worn-out futon bed I started using when I moved in with my son Cody with a new double bed air mattress. I put an electric blanket under this mattress that perfectly heats the mattress to a comfortable warm temperature to sleep on. It is an inconvenience, but much more manageable or cheaper than building a new house to suit my disabilities. I learned that I have no advertising or marketing skills, so I have no expectations of receiving anything from this book other than the satisfaction or joy and happiness that others might find in it! The only one thing I have found difficult to handle of all of the changes in my life is how other people are not able to accept that I was created to be able to thrive on what has happened to me and I work more efficiently and productively now on computers than before losing the majority of the right side of my brain! This is driven by my passion to do the most good possible for others now nothing for my own benefit or prosperity! I write this after I amazed myself that I successfully renamed 1,189 .MP3 files for the KJV Bible in one day followed by updating the start of each of these audio files to include the book being read in the equivalent of one day! I must complete the .html pages for the NIV Bible before I continue on the KJV audio files for the daily devotional readings WebApp. I developed the pages for this WebApp readings to include both the audio files; playable in the browser with an html5 audio player that is located at the top of the page above the text of the reading in a separate in-line frame page, so one may scroll through the text following listening to the reading to pause the audio if anything catches your attention. I have estimated that by the time I complete all of the pages for the KJV Bible, I will have developed 32,000 plus files of both .MP3 and .html formats for an estimated 220 Gb of data on the www.ondemandwisdom.com website I accept that I am nothing in comparison to what others could learn from Jesus Christ through the Christ's on demand daily devotional WebApp!

www.ondemandwisdom.com/Daily_Devotional_Readings.htm

Manitoba Hydro has also benefited from my improvement in working on computers now. A co-worker asked me if I would update a list of CS Orders in a spreadsheet she would E-mail me. I had never performed any work with CS Orders before this, so I had to learn this first. The instructions my co-worker provided were completely incorrect and she was out of the office on the Friday I finally received the required authorization to start the required transaction. A group of other co-workers determined the correct actions required to correctly update the orders. I surprised myself when I completed updating 390 CS orders in 1.92 hours! I will not let myself use having four massive hemorrhagic strokes as an excuse for not being able to work as well as I did before, but in reality I have used what has happened to me be a positive improvement over how I worked before losing the majority of the right half of my brain! I had always found the most efficient and productive way to complete whatever work I have to do. I have had no change in this respect to my work abilities. It is being half blind now that has forced me to work like I do to be so efficient and productive, because of the extreme challenge I have following the mouse moving on the screen, I do all of this work mouse free or in a way to not need to move the mouse, but just click on it in the example of renaming 1,189 .MP3 files in one day!I must conclude this chapter with the following:

I have managed to handle the changes of living with only one full usable hand since December 2002 so well, I think I would be taking a brief step backwards now if I were to miraculously regain the sense of touch in my left hand, because I do not remember how I would use two hands now to do everything in life! I would be starting over learning how to use two hands again!

CHAPTER EIGHT:

The Positives of Being Thankful

First and foremost, I learned the true meaning, value and power of love after I finally said from my heart, "Thank you Jesus for saving my life in January 2006, when the half-ton truck's side rear view mirror was so close to my left cheek, I felt the wind from it on the half physically dead side of my body, which only feels pain or super hyper sensations. I was standing there trembling, thinking I would have been decapitated if I had completed stepping onto Kirkbridge Drive to cross over to the north side. My second greatest thankfulness is for the sense of touch on the right side of my body: for without it, I would not be able to survive now living independently being half physically dead. Losing the sense of touch on the entire left side of my body has made me realize and accept that the sense of touch is probably the most taken for granted of our senses. After all, without the sense of touch, I have no fine manual dexterity in my left-hand, which disables me from doing just about everything with it other than holding something big enough like a bottle to open the lid with my right-hand.

Without the sense of touch, you cannot just pick up a small object even though you can see that your fingers are on both sides of the object, as my occupational therapist said I could do. I also do not require experiencing the most embarrassing event that ever occurred in my life, which was having my common law spouse Teri or my brother Mark wipe my butt after a bowel movement when I was in the hospital in 2002 . This after miraculously surviving four bleeds in my brain due to burst aneurysms. With the sense of touch in my right-hand and having learned well enough to move with a half physically dead body, I can manage on my own wiping my butt after a bowel movement. Thank you, dear I Am, for making me get the paper ripped off the roll on the perforation thank you for doing that for me one hundred percent, not letting my incompetence show through the slightest. Thank you, dear I Am, for the sense of touch in my right hand enabling me to do this myself, not requiring someone else to do it for me, but even with the sense of touch. Thank you, dear I Am, for doing it for me to not let my incompetence show through the slightest.

I did not accept the page or so of this chapter my editor deleted, but did refrain from including the exact details of how I say thank you for absolutely everything in my life now. In September of 2004, I joined the Manitoba Hydro five-pin co-ed bowling league. I knew I was not able to skate, so thought bowling might be a suitable sport to get involved in. I was shocked that I was able to throw the bowling ball down the lane (though somewhat uncomfortably), having to bend my right knee while throwing the ball with my right hand. I immediately said, "Thank you, Jesus, for making it possible for me to enjoy bowling as my sport to participate in now with my disabilities." In addition, I said in my heart that I would not practice bowling, to try to become the best bowler, as I practiced to be the best I possibly could be in every other sport I ever participated in. I was often embarrassed cheering for a strike or a spare I thought was made, only to see the left two pin still standing. This was not only for balls I had thrown, but for my teammate's balls as well.

I knew nothing about team scoring in bowling and never did take the time to check it out, because I had no thoughts of bowling well enough to be on a winning team to enjoy bowling as the sport I now could participate in. I rarely looked at the scoreboard while bowling to even know what frame I was in, but only knew it was the tenth frame by my teammates' hollering at me to strike out . My average at the end of the first year was 169; I had no idea if this was good, bad or average and did not care to find out. I was happy with my bowling, even though our team, the Crips, were the skunk team of the league that first year and the following two . It did not take long for me to accept my inabilities to bowl well in my condition, and it could therefore only be Jesus Christ making me throw a ball well enough to make a strike or a spare. I began to thank Jesus for every ball well-thrown for doing it for me and for every not well-thrown ball, for letting me throw it myself; for allowing me to know my abilities throwing a bowling ball and how much better I bowled if Jesus threw it for me . Jesus did not let me bowl a perfect game like I wanted to, but let my average decline every year after the great first year of 169 . I had the occasional turkey in the first of year bowling, but rarely even had a strike in the 2008-2009 (my last year bowling). Thank God, our team could not have won any more. We were the Grand Aggregate Winners and the Winners of the Year!

Here are the grand aggregate and winners of the year bowling trophies!!
(key this into the command line of your browser to view the
image on-line! www.keithlistoe.ca/26-04-09_1305.jpg)

My teammates all joked and laughed with me at what had become my norm of bowling in the last year: I would get a spare, and then my first ball of the next frame would be in the right gutter. I basically was a spud bowler, rarely getting more than fifteen in a frame in my last year. Because I am a perfectionist, I have learned through this type of being thankful that I only complete anything perfectly if Jesus does it for me; but if Jesus lets me do it on my own, it is so evident how incompetent I am at doing most everything in life . But thank God, for the attitude I was given to not stop, quit or give up at whatever I decide to do.

I'm not afraid to start doing something because I do not know how to do it, thinking I might make a mistake or be unsuccessful. That led to me thinking that I had a great day if I learned something new. I have had no shortage of learning new things or how to do everything in my life now only having one full usable hand. I can honestly write: I have lived a great life since December 2002, when I miraculously survived four bleeds in my brain due to burst aneurysms. I suffered from depression in my early teens because I was so small and skinny; but now I am completely thankful for that, because if I were big-boned and bulky with muscle, I would not be able to dress myself. Without the use of my left-hand, I am not able to undo or do up the buttons on my right cuff of my long-sleeved shirts. Because I am skinny enough, my right-hand can slip through the shirt sleeve cuff buttoned up, putting it on or taking it off! Exodus 3 verses 14 and 15, 14: And God said to Moses, "I AM WHO I AM." And He said, "Thus you shall say to the children of Israel, 'I AM has sent me to you.'" 15 Moreover God said to Moses, "Thus you shall say to the children of Israel: 'The LORD God of your fathers, the God of Abraham, the God of Isaac, and the God of Jacob, has sent me to you . This is My name forever, and this is My memorial to all generations.'"

This has led to me say thank you each evening while getting undressed and each morning as I get dressed. For example, thank you, dear I Am, for making me undo all of the buttons or snaps on my shirt and getting it untucked from my pants. Thank you dear I Am, for making me get the snaps on the right cuff undone using my teeth, or if it is a button up cuff, Thank you dear I Am, for making me get my right hand out of the cuff and sleeve. Thank you dear I Am, for making me get my left-hand out of the cuff and sleeve. Thank you dear I

Am, for making me get the shirt off me without dropping it on the floor. Thank you dear I Am, for making me get the shirt hung up on the clothes hanger. Thank you dear I Am, for making me hang the clothes hanger up successfully on the rod in the closet. Thank you dear I Am, for making me get the belt undone, pulled out of my pants and hung up over the back of the chair. Thank you dear I Am, for making me get the zipper undone on my pants. Thank you dear I Am for making me get the button undone on my pants. Thank you dear I Am, for making me get the long john sweats and pants pulled down off my buttocks, to be able to sit down to complete getting undressed . Thank you dear I Am for making me get the pant leg off my right foot and leg. Thank you dear I Am, for not letting the long john sweats get entangled around my right foot. Thank you dear I am, for making me get the long john sweats pant leg untucked from my right sock . Thank you dear I am, for making me get the sock off my right foot. Thank you dear I am, for making me get the sock placed on the back of the chairs for the night. Thank you dear I am, for making me get my left leg over my right knee. Thank you dear I am, for making me get the pant leg off my left foot and leg. Thank you dear I am, for making me throw the pants on top of the bed, freeing my right-hand to complete getting undressed. Thank you dear I am, for not letting the long john sweats get entangled around my left foot. Thank you dear I am, for making me get the long john sweats pant leg untucked from my left sock . Thank you dear I am, for making me get the sock off my left foot. Thank you dear I am, for making me put the sock on top of the back of the chairs for the night. Thank you dear I am, for making me get the long john sweats pant leg off my left foot and leg . Thank you dear I am, for making me flip the long john sweats up into my lap to find the front center of them to place on the side of my footrest stool . Thank you dear I am, for making me get the pants straightened out and folded on the bed. Thank you dear I am for making me get the pants onto the clothes hanger. Thank you dear I am, for making me get the clothes hanger with my pants on them hanging up in the closet. Thank you dear I am, for making me step successfully into the tub. Thank you dear I am, for making me turn the water on perfectly to the desired hot temperature. Thank you dear I am for making me step success-fully out of the tub. Thank you dear I am, for making me have a safe successful shower with no problems, hassles, complications or inconveniences. Thank you dear I am for making me pick the towel up successfully on the correct side. Thank you dear I am for making me swing the towel around my head, shoulders and back. Thank you dear I am, for making me get my face dried with the corner of the towel around my head. Thank you dear I am for making me flip the other end of the towel up onto my right shoulder, enabling me to grab the corner of it with my right-hand to dry my face again and the rest of my body . Thank you dear I am, for making me open my left-hand to be able to dry it inside and out. Thank you dear I am, for making me hold my left-hand up high enough to dry my left underarm. Thank you dear I am, for making me bend down far enough to dry my left calf, ankle and foot. Thank you dear I am, for making me bend down far enough to dry my right calf, ankle and foot without pulling the towel off my shoulders and neck . Thank you dear I am, for making me get my left foot and leg through the shorts leg hole, while leaning on the wall . Thank you dear I am, for making me get my right foot and leg through the shorts leg hole, while leaning on the wall . Thank you dear I am, for making me get my shorts on me, while leaning on the wall without having to sit down on the toilet . Thank you dear I am, for the sense of touch in my right hand to feel the light switch to turn the light on in the dark. Thank you dear I am, for making me get my left thumb inside my fist. Thank you dear I am, for making me get my left-hand through the sleeve. Thank you dear I am, for making me get my right-hand through the sleeve. Thank you dear I am, for making me see the back of the neck-hole indicator. Thank you dear I am for making me get my head through the neck hole. Thank you dear I am for making me get the T-shirt on me no problems, hassles, complications or inconveniences without a damp sticky body . Thank you for doing that for me! Thank you dear I am for making me get my left-hand through the sleeve and cuff. Thank you dear I am for making me get the snaps on the right cuff done up before I put my right-hand in the sleeve. Thank you dear I am for making me get my right-hand through the sleeve and cuff done up. Thank you dear I am for making me get the shirt on me successfully. Thank you dear I am for making me get the buttons or snaps done up successfully and in the correct alignment at the start, so I do not need to redo them . Thank you dear I am for making me get the shirt tucked into my shorts for me. Thank you dear I am for making me get my left leg over my right knee. Thank you dear I am for making me get my left foot and leg

successfully through the long john sweats pant leg . Thank you dear I am for making me get my right foot and leg successfully through the long john sweats pant leg, so smoothly and easily not making my right knee snap loudly making lots of noise without any pain! . Thank you dear I am for doing that all for me 100 percent, and not letting my incompetence show through the slightest! Thank you dear I am for making me pick that sock up successfully on the first attempt. Thank you dear I am for making me get my left leg over my right knee. Thank you dear I am for making me get the sock on my left foot for me, so smoothly and easily. Thank you dear I am, for doing that for me 100 percent, not letting my incompetence show through the slightest. Thank you dear I am for making me get the long john sweats pant leg tucked into the sock on my left foot for me . Thank you dear I am for making me pick that sock up success- fully on the first attempt. Thank you dear I am for just letting my right knee snap loudly making lots of noise, without any pain . Thank you dear I am for making me get the sock on my right foot for me, so smoothly and easily. Thank you dear I am for doing that all for me 100 percent, and not letting my incompetence show through the slightest!. Thank you dear I am for making me get the long john sweat pant leg tucked into the sock on my right foot for me, so smoothly and easily . Thank you dear I am, for doing that for me 100 percent, not letting my incompetence show through the slightest. Thank you dear I am for making me get my left leg over my right knee. Thank you dear I am for making me get my left foot and leg through the pant leg, so smoothly and easily. Thank you dear I am for making me get my right foot and leg through the pant leg, so smoothly and easily, not making my right knee snap loudly making lots of noise without any pain!. Thank you dear I am for doing that all for me 100 percent, and not letting my incompetence show through the slightest! Thank you dear I am for making me get the button done up on my pants. Thank you dear I am for making me get the zipper done up on my pants. Thank you dear I am for making me get the shorts and long john sweats tucked into my pants. Thank you dear I am for making me get the belt through the belt loops for me. Thank you dear I am, for making me get the belt done up for me. Thank you dear I Am, for the sense of touch to be able to get myself dressed;

but even so with the sense of touch, thank you for doing it all for me to not let my incompetence show through in the slightest! In addition, I live pain free now and my body functions as well as we are created to function . I know from talking to my brother Mark during his terminal illness, how my life would be if my body did not function as we are created to function: I am thankful for every natural functioning of my body; thank you for making my body function as you created it to, by expelling gas from my body through my mouth or my anus for my comfort, health and well-being; thank you for making my body function as you created it to, by expelling urine and feces, stool from my body through my penis and anus for my comfort, health and well-being! Thank God I was at home in my apartment the first time I experienced the non-complete void of urine, but I must squeeze very deeply on the urinary tract on the left side of my groin to complete the void of urine before I sit down, which forces the completion of the void of urine; it is not a small quantity remaining, but enough to soak my entire left leg and I received no warning from a doctor that this might happen. I can only guess it is because they have no experience or knowledge of the consequences of the amount of brain damage I miraculously survived, by the grace of God, the Father, the Son, Jesus Christ and the Holy Spirit. Because of the challenge I now face swallowing any liquid, I say thank you after each successful swallow of water while taking my vitamins and or nutritional supplements after each meal for the safe and successful swallows of the mouth full of water. I begin by saying: Thank you dear I Am, for making me stop pouring the water into the glass in time to not overfill it, spilling the water. Thank you dear I Am, for making me get the lid off the bottle for me. Thank you dear I Am, for making me dump all of the vitamins and or nutri-tional supplements into the lid without any spilling onto the table. Thank you dear I Am, for making me pick that pill up successfully on the first attempt. Thank you dear I Am, for making me swallow that pill on the first attempt. Thank you dear I Am, for making me have safe and successful swallows of that mouth full of water. This is repeated until I complete all 10 of my vitamins and or nutritional supplements, then thank you dear I Am, for making me have a safe and successful guzzle of all the remaining water . Thank you dear I Am, for making me to get the remaining vitamins and or nutritional supplements into the bottle without any spilling onto the table. Thank you dear I Am, for making me get the lid on tightly, only needing to use my right-hand, but after supper it is thank you dear I am, for making me to get the lid on the empty bottle tightly only needing to use my right-hand! . Thank you dear I Am, for making me get the steam heated pie plate cover out of the micro wave into the cupboard without burning my fingers using this thick cloth towel. Thank you dear I Am, for making me close the cupboard door in the proper order of sequence before taking the plate out of the micro wave. Thank you dear I Am, for making me get the micro wave door closed using my left-hand, not too hard and not having to push it twice! Thank you dear I Am, for making me carry that steam heated plate of food out to the table without burning my fingers using this thick cloth towel.

But my brother Mark has set the stakes very high on being thankful, as per the following details of him. He thought I was such a good example of not letting what has happened to me stop me or make me quit or give up, but I live pain free from all that I was required to experience to make me change to a true giving from my heart love for my neighbor as myself . Jesus told us what we should do to have everlasting life with him and the Father after the end of the ages.

I took the chance on receiving a phone call that I had been selected to buy a nine-day, eight-night south Florida vacation package, including a three-day, two-night Caribbean cruise from Fort Lauderdale, Florida to Nassau, Bahamas for two from Ramada Plaza Resorts, in the spring of 2007. Thank God, my then common law spouse Teri refused to go on this vacation with me, and I phoned my brother Mark to ask if he wanted to go. Thank God, Mark had just started using a new prescription medication that provided him the ability to eat more food for increased strength and energy. I bought the required flights for Mark and me, because the times I could get using my Aeroplan points did not suit Mark's condition of living with terminal carcinoid tumor cancer since 2000. I learned on the first day of this vacation when we went to the beach in Fort Lauderdale that Mark's small intestine was so blocked by the tumors that it had burst and pushed out the lower right side of his abdomen, forming a natural colostomy. His intestines remained so blocked up that his doctor cut a second colostomy on the left side of his lower abdomen, but the cut was too close to the natural colostomy. Mark could not put on two adult-size colostomy bags, but had to use one adult bag and one junior bag. Thank God, I discovered that being thankful makes you happy: here is the URL:

(Key this into the command line of your browser to view on-line www.youtube.com/watch?v=oHv6vTKD6lg)

CHAPTER NINE:

The Positives of Bawling Uncontrollably

My first experience of bawling uncontrollably was only in a discussion with my brother Mark after our grandfather Ole Listoe's funeral in 1983. We were building our house at the time and everyone just sat around after his funeral sobbing and crying. Mark and I left to continue working on the house, saying to each other, if you are going to cry at a funeral, cry like you mean it, not just weepy sobbing crying. We then agreed that Grandpa Listoe lived a great life. We should be having a party to celebrate his great life and everything we learned from him, not sitting around crying. Let's be sure they have a party after our funerals.

I must say that my first true time bawling uncontrollably was in 2006. It was not me only, but by being filled with the Holy Spirit to speak in tongues that was verbally expressed as uncontrollable bawling. I never imagined it was possible to bawl so hard and uncontrollably, as the truest deepest innermost expression of my love and thankfulness to Jesus Christ. I was struggling to remain sitting in my chair in front of my desk. I was reading the introduction booklet to the course to become an associate member of the Order of Saint Luke the physician. I had started reading a paragraph titled "being thankful." I do not have this booklet anymore to quote it word for word, but it was, if you are saying thank you, don't just say thank you from your lips, but say thank you from your heart.

I said from my heart, "You know me, Jesus, that I am saying thank you and I love you from my heart." I immediately began bawling uncontrollably, harder than I had ever imagined it was possible to cry. I was completely comfortable bawling like this, because I knew the reason and it made me feel exceedingly good. I thought, *I would not be embarrassed to bawl like this in public, because I know the true meaning of such intense uncontrollable bawling now;* but I accept that the Holy Spirit will not move me to bawl like this in public. Because of my condition, anyone who sees me would for sure think I was having a seizure!

My second experience was on November 16, 2008 with my brother Mark at his home in Prince Albert, Saskatchewan. I arrived there the previous night and asked Mark if he wanted to see the spreadsheet I had told him I was developing in 2007 when I took him on a nine day, eight night south Florida vacation package, which included a three day, two night Caribbean cruise from Fort Lauderdale, Florida to Nassau, Bahamas. He said, "I really want to, but I am not able, because the computer is upstairs and I do not have the strength to go up and down the stairs." I did not think of it at all while I was with Mark in PA, but this was the first time that either of us was not able to do what the other asked, which killed Mark more than living with a terminal illness.

The next morning, I was sitting on the sofa and Mark came walking up to me with only a pair of shorts on, seeing his body was nothing but skin and bones and I immediately felt like bawling uncontrollably; but I refrained and went into the kitchen to talk to Mom about this. She immediately said, "That would not be a good thing to do right now." I immediately knew what I needed to do with my need to bawl uncontrollably for Mark. I walked up to Mark as he was sitting on his bed. I wrapped my arms around him and started lowering my head onto his left shoulder, saying, "Mark, I just need your shoulder to bawl on for you." And I burst out bawling uncontrollably slightly less than my first time bawling uncontrollably while expressing my love and thankfulness to Jesus Christ. I bawled for quite some time and Mark wrapped his arms around me saying, "Thank you Keith for being comfortable enough to express your feelings for me like you are. You have made me feel the best I ever have through all I have gone through."

I now know that this was my grieving for my brother Mark personally before he died from his terminal illness. I cannot even imagine the pain he had to tolerate continuously for eight years. He had intolerable pain in his lower abdomen starting in 2000, but the doctor was unable to determine any reason for the pain until exploratory surgery was performed in 2004, which concluded he had carcinoid tumor cancer in his small intestines. I immediately phoned Mark on hearing this. He said "Keith, I know this might be terminal, but I will not let this kill me before I die!

I learned on our trip to Florida in December 2007 that his intestines were so blocked that it had burst and pushed through his lower right abdomen forming a natural colostomy. The doctor had to cut a second colostomy on the left side of his abdomen, so he required wearing two colostomy bags at the same time; and because they were too close together he had to wear one adult bag and one junior bag. Mark's definition of letting this kill him was to let himself cry for himself or feel bad because of what was happening to him or think that he was too ill to do whatever he wanted or needed to do! He felt the best he ever had, because he knew me so well that I would bawl uncontrollably for him if I saw the condition of his body not being strong enough to go up and down the stairs. I can best describe his body was decomposing from the inside out.

I asked Mom at his funeral. "Why did you say it was not the best thing to do right now?" She answered, "Mark was told in October that he only had three days left to live. I immediately thought, *I know what Mark said to the doctor,* but I did not say anything to Mom at his funeral. In September of 2009, I was talking to his widow Veryl and asked her if it was okay if I asked her if this is what Mark said to the doctor in October when he told Mark that he only had three days to live." She said "Sure, what did he say?" I said, "Don't you tell me when I'm going to die, you just hydrate me, clean out my innards and I will die when I die. I will not let you kill me now with your words!" Veryl asked, "When did Mark tell you what he said to the doctor because those are Mark's exact words?" I said, "Mark never told me anything, I knew nothing about him being told this until I asked Mom at his funeral, why she didn't think it was a good thing for me to bawl in front of Mark in November 2008. Veryl replied, "You and Mark really did know each other." There is nothing more positive you could do for someone with a terminal illness than bawling uncontrollably for them before they die from the illness, but if you miss grieving for them in person before they die, be sure to bawl uncontrollably at their funeral. I must conclude that it was this type of bawling that was so significant in Jesus' day that it was written about in John 11 verses 35 and 36: [35] Jesus wept. [36] Then the Jews said, "See how He loved him."

CHAPTER TEN:

The Value of Complaining

I find that most people are negative towards the weather, only complaining, which I think is a complete waste of time and energy, as no one can do anything about it. I just look outside for the day, dress accordingly and enjoy the day. I will never let the weather set my mood for the day. On thinking more about the weather, I believe it is one of those situations of mind over matter. If you think it is too cold out, your subconscious will make you feel cold, so your conscious mind's thinking is correct in making you feel good that you really know yourself and how the weather is. But if you think it is cold, but you can dress warm enough to go out in it, you will go out and be just fine, not cold at all. After all, you did what you wanted to do. In addition, you feel good that you really know yourself.

In the saying I used earlier, *Mind over Matter*, the matter is one's own body, as your mind does have complete control over the body either negative or positive. The choice is each person's, which way they will control their body, negative or positive. It's not with the conscious mind, but for sure, the subconscious controls the body. Moreover, a person's conscious thoughts affect how the subconscious will control the body to ensure the conscious mind's thinking is correct. This may be a new law of the universe. "The subconscious wants to guarantee that the conscious mind's thinking is always correct, either positive or negative; but it will only truly guarantee negative thinking." As such, one becomes what they think, positive or negative. I have never seen a person complaining with a smile on their face. I therefore doubt complaining makes you feel joyful and happy. I conclude that complaining is a complete waste of time and energy, of no value of any kind! Put a smile on your face and stop complaining!

I do not complain as a general rule in my life, but there is something that happened to me when I was on the step-down unit in the Health Sciences Center Hospital in 2002 that I feel justifies me writing this complaint, for other people's benefit and well-being who might be in a hospital. I was lying in bed and a female nurse walked up to my left side, grabbed my left-hand and pulled extremely hard to sit me up, and this hurt my left shoulder intensely. I called for Dr. Daniels to tell her this happened and to have her check my shoulder for any injury, but she flat out refused to look at my shoulder insisting it did not happen and that I only felt pain on my left side because I had suffered a stroke. I might have suffered a stroke, but I know that the proper way to lift a patient into a sitting position is to put your hand under their back and ask them to sit up as you assist them, by lifting on their back. No doctor or physiotherapist ever looked or felt my left shoulder. I thought it would be looked at by Dr. Nemith at the Pan Am Clinic; but he only told me to lift my left-hand and my shoulder snapped loud enough for him to hear it across the room and he said, "That is your rotator cuff."

I went over to my friend Terry Rempel's one evening to use their swimming pool to assist me lifting my left-hand in the water; in the summer of 2005, and a friend of his was there from overseas. He was a therapist of some kind, but not working here in Canada. He looked at and felt my shoulder, telling me it had been partially dislocated, because he could still feel a space in the shoulder joint. It is impossible to prove this now though, because my shoulder was dislocated and the shoulder joint ball crushed by the SUV impacting me on December 10, 2005, and it is now an artificial shoulder joint. But thank God the doctor did not touch my left knee other than showing me how it could bend in all directions after the SUV impacted me and I was released from the hospital on December 22, 2005, wearing a G2 brace on my left leg. I was fully mobile and relatively pain free; oh, the grace of God, for his glory, power, might and love to be revealed through me. I have sufficient reasons to write that my personal doctor is insane, because she thinks it is more reasonable for me to perform self-surgery to castrate myself than accepting my suggestion for an alternative that I know is impossible for me to do, though it would have provided me the desired results the same as if I were to castrate myself except no loss of testosterone.

In addition, she thinks that I must continue to take the anti-seizure medication even though the only guarantee she can give me is that it will damage my liver. I think she thinks this is okay because God heals my liver perfectly, as proven to her repeatedly by the results of my three-month blood tests that continue to come back perfect. I made my own decision to stop taking the anti-seizure medication, but I trust God that I will not have any future seizures if I do not take any painkiller medications either.

I must include the first complaint I ever verbally expressed in 2009. The SAP Support Services Department was the first department to move into 360 Portage Avenue in 2008, before the construction had been 100 percent completed on the atriums. My co-workers said, "It is going to be tough for you, Keith, because you cannot bring your personal heater into the new building. I did not even waste my time or energy responding to such comments, because I would not know if I needed my personal heater. I was required to work in the old drafty building at 820 Taylor Avenue, until after I had worked in the new building to know how it was for my personal comfort now in my condition of living half physically dead that I feel frozen constantly on the left side of my body; but it is unbearable if there is the slightest cool draft on my body. But I do not expect anyone else to be able to understand this, so I do not verbally complain about it; I just do what I can to lessen the discomforts I do have.

The complaint I verbally expressed was during a coffee break, as I sat and listened to all of my co-workers complaining about the temperature and noise in the new office building. I said, "You have all finally given me something I will complain about." They all responded with, "You never complain about anything." I completed my complaint, "I have to sit here and listen to you all complaining!" I only had one day that the temperature was uncomfortably cool on the floor, when John Kirby left his window open overnight, but I did not complain. Instead, I closed the window to let the temperature slowly stabilize. I do not join in the complaining coffee breaks anymore, but rather use my break time to run the stairs and to close my eyes in the quiet room over my lunch break.

Sometimes my eyes are sore and a headache begins from staring at my computer screen too long. When I hear healthy normal people complaining, it only makes me think of saying, *try living in my shoes for a day and then see what you have to complain about.* To be sure non-TBI and other TBI people can understand that it is only by the grace of God, I am able to be as joyful and happy as I am now. I have come up with the following simulation of living with a half physically dead body. It involves the non-dominant side of your body, i.e.: your left side if you are right-handed and vice versa. I know how impossible it is for me to do one of the listed things continuously all day long, I would not recommend you try doing more than one at a time for an extended length of time; but in my reality if I wanted to appear non TBI or fully recovered, I would need to do the entire list continuously all day long!

As mentioned previously, my left foot is turned inward as I take a step, so to simulate, try turning your left toe inward as you take a step. My left shoulder hangs down lower than normal, resulting in me having to consciously think about lifting it up to a normal position. To simulate, try holding your left shoulder down in a lower than normal position. My head is tilted over my left shoulder. I have no idea it is until I start to feel pain in my left shoulder and back. I must consciously think about tilting my head slightly over my right shoulder to know it is not tilted over my left shoulder. To simulate, try tilting your head over your left shoulder.

My left arm does not swing as I walk, but is motionless hanging on my left side. If I try to make it swing like normal, it messes up my walking that I must concentrate completely on by moving my left foot and leg to take a step. To simulate try holding your left arm motionless as you walk.

I do not have the sense of touch in my left-hand, making it near impossible to use my left-hand for anything more than gross manual tasks. It is difficult for me to hold something big enough like my toothbrush, as I have to put it into my left-hand with my right-hand to squeeze the toothpaste onto the bristles. To simulate, try holding something in your left- hand all day to only have your right-hand to do everything with.

I had these ideas of how a normal, non-TBI person could simulate having to live as a stroke survivor after a man said, "If you know that your left foot is turned inward, just straighten it out." I have the normal functioning right side of my body that I was able to test my holding your shoulder down simulation to know that the moment I thought about something else I was required to do, my right shoulder was back in the normal position. I know from experiencing my entire left side of my body tightening up and becoming painful, from my head tilted over my left shoulder, while I was in the hospital in 2003 before I was discharged. Be careful if you do decide to try this simulation. Now I know the reason for this pain. If I feel the pain beginning, I know to tilt my head slightly over my right shoulder and the pain disappears.

I must conclude that I do not complain the least about everything that has happened to me, because God was justified in abasing me by making my entire physical brain swell to equal the size of my swollen thoughts of myself. After all, I was living such an evil, wicked and sinful life that was unthinkably rebelling against my parents' strict Christian upbringing. I am thankful that I did not experience the unjust human prison system due to my sinful living, because I know that I am not a strong enough person to have survived it. [1] Chronicles 19 verse 13: 'And David said to Gad, "I am in great distress. Please let me fall into the hand of the LORD, for His mercies *are* very great; but do not let me fall into the hand of man."' I am a strong enough person to survive the amount of changes in my life. becoming a content eight-year-old man with forty-three years' experience, half physically dead miracle man walking: all by the grace of God that he did not leave my side when I walked away from him living my sinful life. It could only be by the Holy Spirit sustaining me now that I am able to survive.

CHAPTER ELEVEN:

Negatives of Personal Possessions

Personal possessions cause nothing but worry, anxiety, stress, fear and discontentment. The greater number of personal possessions one owns only increases your worry, anxiety, stress and fear! Isaiah 55 verses 1 and 2:[1] "Ho, everyone who thirsts, come to the waters; and you who have no money, come buy and eat. Yes, come, buy wine and milk without money and without price. 2 Why do you spend money for what is not bread? And your wages for what does not satisfy? Listen diligently to me, and eat what is good, and let your soul delight itself in abundance."

CHAPTER TWELVE:

Positive Personal Possessions

If a personal possession is required for survival, it is positive.

Ezekiel 44 verse[28] "It shall be, in regard to their inheritance, *that I am* their inheritance. You shall give them no possession in Israel, for I *am* their possession.

CHAPTER THIRTEEN

Complete Positive

I have found myself in situations trying to think of an idea or way to accomplish the task at hand. In the four examples below, they were not simply wants, but needs. Not critical needs, but of high importance to me.

1 - My common law spouse, Teri, had always carried the blue recycle bin and garbage to the curb on garbage day for pick up. She was gone for a two-week vacation, leaving me at home alone, not of any concern. I had not tried to twist tie the black garbage bags yet or carry anything of much weight with my non-feeling left-hand and artificial left shoulder. During this two-week period, there was a garbage day. My first concern was getting the garbage out to the curb. The challenge would be to hold the bag in the air with my left hand twisting the bag, then twisting on the twist tie. Once tied, I had no problem carrying the bags to the curb. Next was the blue bin. I was somewhat hesitant to try carrying this bin with my left-hand. I stood there looking at it for a time finally saying to myself, 'I have no option; I **will** do it with one hand'. I slid it off the counter in the garage holding it tight against my right hip and walking to the curb. It took another moment of hesitation before I slide it down my leg to the ground.

In November 2005, my Mom suggested I write a nightcap of my day's activities. I started doing this soon, adding many more recipients to my cap list. I started with my immediate family, soon adding aunts, uncles and cousins, naming this new list to extended family.

2 - I started to write one afternoon that we all gather at the next family function to brainstorm for an idea to enable me to know where the void of my left field of vision starts. I wanted to include an idea in this cap to initiate some brainstorming remotely. I was thinking and thinking, mainly how confident the great thinking brains in my cap list would for sure do well at thinking of a solution to enable me to know where this void begins. Without knowing where it begins or where my vision stops, I do not know when to turn my head to see further to my left.

After quite some time thinking with no results, I changed my thinking to **I will** think of an idea and immediately I did. As such, only complete positive thoughts mean something, but you must think you will do it. This is thinking you have achieved success before starting; you leave yourself no option but to be successful, hence you are. My idea in this e-mail received no further thoughts from my cap list. My son recently suggested I have a hologram image or such put in my glasses to indicate where this void of my field of vision begins. Thinking of, "will" brings to mind the statement *where there's a will, there's a way.* My previous thinking of the word will in this statement was having great desire or great enough want there's a way. Now I know it is how you will achieve the task at hand simply by thinking you will! Further, if you want to do something, don't just say I will **try**, but be more assertively confident and say **I will do** this.

3 - In 2006, I was asked if I would like to give my motivational speech at the ITS conference. I said yes. A couple of days later, I was told the theme for the conference is overcoming obstacles. I immediately thought, *I do not use those words in my speech anywhere.* I must rewrite a section of it to emphasize this theme. I thought for a couple of days with no results. I made the decision to change my thinking to **I will** think of the words to emphasize overcoming obstacles. Almost immediately, I thought of an idea to add to my speech.

This idea grew over time, eventually becoming the book, *The Human Mind Positively Can*

The power of the subconscious! But the idea itself has become Chapter Fourteen: The Most Common Obstacle in this book.

4 - My brother Mark and I lived in a small basement suite in Saskatoon, Sk. in the early 1980s. Then sometime in 1982, we received a letter from the owner of the property stating that he was going to put the house up for sale and it would be in our best interest if we found an alternate place to live prior to him selling the property. Mark and I discussed our options in-depth. We first thought we would try to purchase the property, however, we soon learned that we required twenty-five percent down to purchase a revenue home. We didn't have any savings as we both were living paycheck to paycheck with nothing extra.

We were also unable to find another suite for even similar rent and neither of us could afford any increase in rent. We then heard an ad that the government of Saskatchewan was providing financial assistance to first-time home buyers, so we thought maybe we could build/buy our first home and receive this assistance. We carefully considered the differences between building vs. buying a home, as neither of us had any experience in the construction industry. As we discussed this, we said to each other, 'We do not have any options, **we will** build ourselves a house to live in!' key this into the command line of your browser to view the details of building this house! www.keithlistoe.ca/346_allegretto_cres.htm

We looked into the option of Nelson Homes, a company that sells semi prefab houses. By this I mean they build all of the walls and deliver them along with all other materials required, to complete the house to the site. The purchaser then needed to assemble all these walls to complete the framing. That includes installing the windows and doors, shingles and siding, then completing the interior/electrical, plumbing and heating, insulation, vapor barrier, drywall, painting, flooring and finishing carpentry, . After much analysis and calculations, we decided on a floor plan from Nelson Homes. We were convinced and confident that we would be able to do this, now we had to convince the Saskatoon Credit Union that we could and get approval for a mortgage.

We finally got our mortgage. After twenty-one applications were rejected, the twenty-second was approved.

CHAPTER FOURTEEN:

The Most Common Obstacle

The biggest, most common obstacle to each human being is our thoughts on whether we think we can or can't achieve the task or not. If you think positively and believe you can, you are much more likely to succeed than if you think you can't, you will not. This follows my thinking that our subconscious wants our conscious thoughts to be correct. It ensures that if we think we can't do something, it will guarantee that we can't, making our conscious thinking correct and vice versa. I truly believe in always thinking positive to ensure my subconscious tries to make me correct with success. I believe this happens so our subconscious always makes our conscious mind's thinking correct, therefore giving our conscious mind the satisfaction that you really know yourself. Even if successful at not doing whatever you thought you were not able to do, you are still happy as you were correct in your thinking of your abilities . Therefore, this gives you a positive thought even though you did not do what you originally wanted to do. This mechanism is how the age-old statement goes: one becomes what you think. The big question becomes, is there a way to control your subconscious thinking? Simply put, it is controlled by your every conscious thought; nothing further is required to control the subconscious to do whatever you want to do or become who you want to be. It's the realization of all your dreams. This is the idea I added to my motivational speech after I had agreed to give it and then told the theme for the conference was overcoming obstacles . I received the following after this ITS Conference in 2006:

2006 ITS Divisional Conference Survey'
Feedback Results For Keith Listoe

The following were comments we received in our feedback survey for the 2006 ITS Divisional Conference. These following comments were under the heading "LIKED BEST":

The speakers. I thought Keith Listoe's speech was especially motivating.

The highlight was Keith's story.

First two speakers of the day were awesome ... brought tears to my eyes. Keith's story was inspiring and made me realize that there are a lot of people with interesting stories working here that I don't know much about.

Good speakers. – my favorites were Keith & the car guys .

I felt for Keith as he shared his vulnerabilities and his determination in healing himself, a never give up attitude, a dissatisfaction with his unplanned for and unexpected status quo.

Loved the motivational speaker series. Truly inspiring. Gary Guller, Keith Listoe, Tom Molinski

I enjoyed both morning speakers. Keith Listoe and Gary Guller.

I found Keith's speech very interesting especially because he is a co-worker and there is a bit of a connection there.

The topics and speakers were very interesting and the personal stories very inspiring. Great choices!

I thought Keith Listoe and Gary Guller were great. I really enjoyed both of their presentations.

The morning was the best. Keith was great to hear from and I thought Gary Guller was a great motivational speaker.

Yes, you couldn't have found a better group of speakers.

All speakers were good but I liked Keith Listoe's speech the best because it was an example of a hydro employee overcoming obstacles.

It was great to hear people's personal stories of how they were able to succeed in overcoming their obstacles.

These following comments were under the heading "LIKED CHANGED":

Although I don't know Keith personally, I thought he had overcome more significant obstacles than Gary and giving so much attention to Gary detracted from Keith's story.

The two morning speakers should have been split up as their topic was the same. I felt it would have been better to have one in the afternoon and one in the morning.

Also, the AM was quite inspirational and the PM wasn't. Not that all talks weren't interesting but the two in the AM were by far more interesting as far as public interest goes . Perhaps one of the inspirational talks could have been in the AM and the other in the PM .

These following comments were under the heading "SUGGESTIONS":

Location was good. Venue was good. Speakers were very well chosen. I personally don't feel that bringing in an external speaker is necessary. Presentations from internal Hydro employees are informative, interesting, and enjoyable.

Gary Guller's speech had me enthralled, and it was really nice to hear Keith's story and to see what a positive person. I immediately   phoned my brother Mark on hearing he had been diagnosed with terminal carcinoid tumor cancer in 2004. He said, "Keith, I know this might be terminal, but I will not let this kill me before I die. . He lived up to his words by buying a motorcycle in 2005, to ride out to the west coast. . He experienced extreme difficulties riding a motorcycle for the hours required, making stops at hotels for days for rests eventually phoning our younger brother Evan in Rocky Mountain House, Ab. To come pick him up with the car. He rested in Rocky until he felt he could continue on to the Columbia ice fields. He made it the 60kms to Nordegg and got a hotel to rest again before heading to Sask Crossing. Key this into the command line of your browser to view the image online: www.keithlistoe.ca/Mark_and_his_motorcycle.jpg My Brother Mark's attitude combined with my own life-long experiences of not letting me think I was ever too ill to do what I wanted or needed to do has made me conclude that the power of how you think controls the results in your life. I feel sorry for people whose parent's instilled in them the thinking that they are not able to do things in life, or people that use injury or illness as an excuse why they can't do things in life, because if you think this way, your subconscious mind will make you feel sick or injured to not be able to do things in your life! I have used what has happened to me to improve my efficiency and productivity working on computers now, opposed to let me think I am unable to work like I did before miraculously surviving four massive hemorrhagic strokes in December 2002! I'm convinced the greatest strength I have for being able to continue working post miraculously surviving four massive hemorrhagic strokes in December 2002, is I love to work! Here are some quotes to support you become what you think: from the audio file strangest_secret by Earle Nightingale recorded in 1956, that I received from Mark Victor Hansen. Key this into your command line of your browser to listen to it on-line: www.keithlistoe.ca/strangest_secret4.mp3

Marcus Aurelius' "A man's life is what his thoughts make of it."

Ralph Waldo Emerson "A man is what he thinks about all day long."

William James "The greatest discovery of my generation is that human beings can alter their lives by altering their attitudes of mind."

Mark 9 verse 23 Jesus said to him, "If you can believe, all things are possible to him who believes."

Norman Vincent Peale "If you think in negative terms, you will get negative results; if you think in positive terms you will achieve positive results, believe and succeed."

William Shakespeare "Our doubts are traitors and make us lose the good we oft might win by fearing to attempt."

George Bernard Shaw "People are always blaming their circumstances for what they are. I don't believe in circumstances, the people who get on in this world, are the people who get up and look for the circumstances they want and if they can't find them, make them."

CHAPTER FIFTEEN:

The End of the Age

Will the age end on a positive note, with the commencement of the restoration of the Earth to its created beauty and splendor? Why is now the time of the end of the age? Mark 13 verse 8: "For nation will rise against nation, and kingdom against kingdom. And there will be earthquakes in various places, and there will be famines and troubles." These *are* the beginnings of sorrows. Mark 13 verses 28 to 30:[28] "Now learn this parable from the fig tree: When its branch has already become tender, and puts forth leaves, you know that summer is near.[29] So you also, when you see these things happening, know that it is near—at the very doors![30] Assuredly, I say to you, this generation will by no means pass away till all these things take place." Hosea 9 verse 7, "The days of punishment have come; the days of recompense have come." Israel knows! The prophet *is* a fool, The spiritual man *is* insane, Because of the greatness of your iniquity and great enmity.

Recent earthquakes and famines,

1. East Africa famine November 8, 2006.
2. Haiti earthquake January 12, 2010.
3. Japan earthquake April 7, 2011.

4. California earthquake August 24 2014.

These are absolute prophesies for the greatest reason. Every human being wants to live the perfect life of complete joy and happiness. We seek, desire and are required to be living now at the end of the age. We have been deceived into thinking we seek and desire to live a life of pleasure, by our love for mammon. But in truth is only a life of worry, anxiety, stress and fear. Consider Revelation 9 verse 4: "They were commanded not to harm the grass of the earth, or any green thing, or any tree, but only those men who do not have the seal of God on their foreheads. The seal of God is the cross of Christ marked on your forehead when you are baptized in the name of the Father and of the Son and of the Holy Spirit." Revelation 9 verses 20 and 21:[20] "But the rest of mankind, who were not killed by these plagues, did not repent of the works of their hands, that they should not worship demons, and idols of gold, silver, brass, stone, and wood, which can neither see nor hear nor walk. [21] And they did not repent of their murders or their sorceries or their sexual immorality or their thefts." In addition, Mark 8 verse 38: "For whoever is ashamed of Me and My words in this adulterous and sinful generation, of him the Son of Man also will be ashamed when He comes in the glory of His Father with the holy angels."

We live in a day and age of great adultery and sinfulness. We live in the most abundant day and age in the history of civilization. We have the means and ability to provide every human being worldwide the total requirements for survival, but unthinkably we refuse to even try to do so. Because of this, God is about to release his wrath on humankind as the end of the age. However, this is also the beginning of the restoration of the Earth to its created beauty, splendor and cleanness; free of all evil and the devastation of living evil lives. Luke 21 verse 23: "But woe to those who are pregnant and to those who are nursing babies in those days! For there will be great distress in the land and wrath upon this people."

A number of the prophets wrote of the beginning of the end of the age, but none of them completed the details of how it will be accomplished. We have been instructed in detail how we must live in order to be resurrected at the end of times to live in this newly restored kingdom of God. We must live life **in** a giving from your heart true love, faith relationship **with** Jesus Christ and giving from your heart love your neighbor as yourself; but accept the truth that we are unable to live righteously, so still require Jesus' healing, saving, grace, mercy and **forgiveness** to be saved unto everlasting life. Isaiah 24 verses 18 and 19: [18] "And it shall be that he who flees from the noise of the fear shall fall into the pit. And he who comes up from the midst of the pit shall be caught in the snare; For the windows from on high are open, and the foundations of the earth are shaken. [19] The earth is violently broken, The earth is split open, The earth is shaken exceedingly." Ezekiel 38 verses 19 and 20: [19] "For in My jealousy and in **the fire of My wrath** I have spoken, 'Surely in that day there shall be **a great earthquake** in the land of Israel, [20] so that the fish of the sea, the birds of the heavens, the beasts of the field, all creeping things that creep on the earth, and all men who are on the face of the earth shall shake at My presence. The mountains shall be thrown down, the steep places shall fall, and **every wall shall fall to the ground**." Malachi 4 verses 1 and 2: [1] "For behold, the day is coming, **Burning like an oven,** And all the proud, yes, all who do wickedly will be stubble. And the day which is coming shall burn them up," Says the LORD of hosts, "That will leave them neither root nor branch. [2] But to you who fear My name The Sun of Righteousness shall arise With healing in His wings; And you shall go out And grow fat like stall-fed calves." Revelation 12 verses 15 and 16: [15] "So the serpent spewed water out of his mouth like a flood after the woman, that he might cause her to be carried away by the flood. [16] But the earth helped the woman, and **the earth opened its mouth** and swallowed up the flood which the dragon had spewed out of his mouth." Mark 13 verse 2: "And Jesus answered and said to him, 'Do you see these great buildings? **Not *one* stone shall be left upon another, that shall not be thrown down.'**" Zechariah 14 verse 4: "And in that day His feet will stand on the Mount of Olives, Which faces Jerusalem on the east. And the Mount of Olives shall be split in two, From east to west, *Making* a very large valley; Half of the mountain shall move toward the north And half of it toward the south. The earth opening its mouth to swallow the water spewed from the dragons mouth is what they all prophesied about."

The earth opening its mouth or splitting open will be the greatest earthquake ever been since creation and will result in not one building left standing worldwide. Hebrews 12, verses 26 and 27: [26] whose voice then shook the earth; but now He has promised, saying, *"Yet once more I shake not only the earth, but also heaven* [27] Now this, *"Yet once more,"* indicates the **removal of those things** that are being shaken, as of things **that are made**, that the things which cannot be shaken may remain. Mark 13 verse 31, "Heaven and **earth will pass away**, but My words will by no means pass away." Haggai 2 verse 21, "Speak to Zerubbabel, governor of Judah, saying, "I will shake heaven and earth." This is not located at the edges of two tectonic plates touching each other, but in the center of a tectonic plate. The water swallowed by the Earth will become a layer of steam encircling the earth just below the surface. There will also be the release of sufficient volcanic ash to completely encircle the Earth in the outer atmosphere. The steam will heat the surface of the Earth like an oven, but it will also burst through in combination with magma at any point on the surface of the Earth heavily contaminated with pollutants causing that surface area to become molten lava. Every ocean and sea will boil. Hebrews 12 verse 29: "For our God is **a consuming fire**. All of this released steam or water vapor will encircle the earth in the outer atmosphere, which will condense on the ash to form the greatest sized hailstones ever hailed on the earth as written Revelation 16 verses 20 and 21, [20] "Then every island fled away, and the mountains were not found. [21] And great hail from heaven fell upon men, *every hailstone* about the weight of a talent. And men blasphemed God because of the plague of the hail, since that plague was exceedingly great."

This hailstorm will be so great that combined with the sun blocked from the ash and steam in the outer atmosphere will become a near instant ice/ash age. The center of every hailstone is volcanic ash. Whatever life on Earth that was not cooked in the oven will be frozen in the ice/ash age. But then this will happen to end the ice/ash age by the brightness of Jesus' great glory on his second coming. Matthew 24 verses 29 and 30: [29] "Immediately after the tribulation of those days the sun will be darkened, and the moon will not give its light; the stars will fall from heaven, and the powers of the heavens will be shaken. [30] Then the sign of the Son of Man will appear in heaven, and then all the tribes of the earth will mourn, and they will see the Son of Man coming on the clouds of heaven with power and great glory. The outer atmosphere will be wiped clean and the sun will shine through, but will pale in comparison to the brightness of Jesus' glory." Revelation 22 verses 1 and 2:[1] "And he showed me a pure river of water of life, clear as crystal, proceeding from the throne of God and of the Lamb. 2 In the middle of its street, and on either side of the river, *was* the tree of life, which bore twelve fruits, each *tree* yielding its fruit every month. And the leaves of the tree *were* for the healing of the nations."

As the ice melts away, there will be left a very thick and fertile layer of volcanic ash soil the world over on which will immediately grow every type of plant and vegetation worldwide. This is the new kingdom of God we will be resurrected onto to kneel before the judgment throne of Jesus Christ. Mark 14 verse 25: "Assuredly, I say to you, I will no longer drink of the fruit of the vine until that day when I drink it new in the kingdom of God." John 11 verses 24 and 25, [24] Martha said to Him, "I know that he will rise again in the resurrection at the last day. [25] Jesus said to her, "I am the resurrection and the life. He who believes in Me, though he may die, he shall live. God ensures that whatever ways Satan tries to make God not true to his word result in the most positive perfect loving world for us humankind to live forevermore on with God." Genesis 9 verses 11 to 16, [11] "Thus I establish My covenant with you: Never again shall all flesh be cut off by the waters of the flood; never again shall there be a flood to destroy the earth." [12] And God said: "This *is* the sign of the covenant which I make between Me and you, and every living creature that *is* with you, for perpetual generations: [13] I set My rainbow in the cloud, and it shall be for the sign of the covenant between Me and the earth. [14] It shall be, when I bring a cloud over the earth, that the rainbow shall be seen in the cloud; [15] and I will remember My covenant which *is* between Me and you and every living creature of all flesh; the waters shall never again become a flood to destroy all flesh. [16] The rainbow shall be in the cloud, and I will look on it to remember the everlasting covenant between God and every living creature of all flesh that *is* on the earth."

ABOUT THE AUTHOR:

I am passionate about convincing humankind of the absolute truth I know of the perfect life of complete joy and happiness; free of worry, anxiety, stress and fear. That we humans seek, desire and are required to be living now at the end of the age, by my true life experiences that for the most part I am completely ashamed of, but I will reveal all; so humankind knows for certain that I am writing the truth! God is just in all that has befallen me!

Nehemiah 9 verse 33: "However You are just in all that has befallen us; For You have dealt faithfully, But we have done wickedly."

1 Corinthians 10 verse 13: "No temptation has overtaken you except such as is common to man; but God is faithful, who will not allow you to be tempted beyond what you are able, but with the temptation will also make the way of escape, that you may be able to bear it." Now that I am content owning only what I require to survive and that worldly material personal possessions only increase your worry, anxiety, stress and fear. I have concluded that the way the majority of parents think they are expressing their love to their children by giving them the latest and greatest material toys as gifts for birthdays and Christmas presents only steals their natural joy and happiness by instilling in them an attitude of want, want and want. Opposed to their naturally born attitude of give, give and give and being content with only what they require to survive! The truth of expressing your love to your children is by providing them everything they require to survive now and forevermore! I thank God for the attitude I was given of being a perfectionist, combined with never

stopping, quitting or giving up at whatever I decide to do; regardless of the number of times I might have to redo something until I think I have completed it perfectly. In addition I am not afraid of starting something because I do not know how to do it, but I can learn from each unsuccessful attempt. Failure to me is to stop quit or give up! I only wish it did not cost so much money to do everything now in my life being half physically dead miracle man living, because I am unable to use most things as is with only one full usable hand, but must have it converted how I determine it will be possible for me to use it using only my right hand! Thank God, I was given the abilities to improvise well enough to come up with the ideas of how to convert all I have required!

Thank God, I was created to be able to handle living half physically dead, miracle man walking to learn the absolute truth that it is only by the Holy Spirit, sustaining me now that I am able to survive independently. I have decided to complete writing my trilogy autobiography.

My First Life My Sinful Lewd Wanton Life
From the beginning, so you and I will know who I was!
My Second Life Miraculous
Against All Odds
By Jesus Christ's unconditional love, saving and
healing, grace mercy and forgiveness!
My Third Life My Near Perfect Life
Content, joyful and happy, but still sinful!

I am sure anyone reading this will be able to understand why I had such a swollen head by the thoughts of myself, because I continue to amaze myself with everything I am still able to do living half physically dead, miracle man walking. For example, I have moved seven times since December of 2002, only the first move in 2004, I did not do much of anything, because I was unsure at the time if I was able to do anything to move. I have increased the amount I did personally on each subsequent move, with moving myself with my adult tricycle and Rubbermaid roughneck storage bins the sixth move from 2501-170 Hargrave Street to 208-936 Chancellor drive, except the big furniture that would not fit in my tricycle basket! The move prior to this I completed with my coolerest moving equipment (Coleman cooler with wheels on one end) on the bus, except my big furniture from 208-936 Chancellor drive to 2501-170 Hargrave Street. I successfully rearrange the big furniture after it is moved into my new apartment by myself one handed. My youngest son, Cody, I live with is constantly amazed at what I successfully do by myself one handed. I do not want to be a disabled burden to anyone now and the Holy Spirit makes me successful at most everything I decide to do by myself now one handed! All things are possible to him who believes!

EPILOGUE:

I rest my case, The Human Mind Positively Can!
The power of the subconscious! But negatively can't be successful!

Thank you for reading my book, for by doing so you assist me in thinking it will be a great success. I am confident I will achieve what I think, for this is my action to achieve my thinking! The concept of the power of the subconscious as written in this my book is my hypothesis only. I must conclude that I did not write this to make anyone feel sorry for me, because I deserved everything that has happened to me; but I was created to thrive on overcoming or doing the impossible. I have had no shortage of impossible situations to overcome since becoming a half physically dead, miracle man walking in December 2002! But I am human and have had enough! I am thankful that I was created to bear witness through my true life experiences of the perfect life of complete joy and happiness we all seek, desire and are required to be living now, at the end of the age.

It has been a very high price to pay to be able to write this book from my true life experiences for humankind's benefit and well-being, now and forevermore! I must conclude that although I feel I have lived a great life, it was not as great as I dreamed my life was going to be as an astronaut. However, I was unable to become an aeronautical and thermodynamic engineer for a basis to become an astronaut. In addition, because my right knee became too

painful playing goal in hockey, I decided not to try playing in the NHL. If I had
known then how well I played goal, I would have played in the NHL regardless
of the pain. I am convinced I would not have been mature enough to handle
the fame and glory of being the best goaltender to ever play in the NHL. But I
took things as they came and saw things as they were and made the most of my
life. I only wish I had learned the truth of the perfect life of complete joy and
happiness in my youth to be able to life this life of complete joy and happiness
my entire life! I feel I must include the numerous other incompletions in my
life, because of the timing of things happening in my life. I built the extra-large
garage at 346 Allegretto Crescent with the plans to complete my 1947 Pontiac
car, but I was transferred to Winnipeg. Mb, before I had time to go back to
Spiritwood to pick it up. My car and my brother Mark's truck were both gone
from the farmyard near Mildred, Sk., where he had placed them both when my
Dad sold the house in Spiritwood, Sk.